Legend and Legacy

A Book about the remembrances of

Isaac Hilliard Terry

Legend and Legacy

A Book about the remembrances of Isaac Hilliard Terry

Malachi 3:16
Then they that feared the Lord spake often one to another:
and the Lord hearkened, and heard it,
and a book of remembrance was written...

Exodus 17:14
Write this for a memorial in a book.

Compiled by

Kenneth Bow

Copyright 2018 by Kenneth Bow

Published 2018.

Printed in the United States of America.

All rights reserved.

No portion of this book may be reproduced, stored in a retrieval system, or transmitted in any form or by any means – electronic, mechanical, photocopy, recording, scanning, or other – except for brief quotations in critical reviews or articles, without the prior written permission of the author.

ISBN 978-1-943650-95-8

Published by BookCrafters, Parker, Colorado.
www.bookcrafters.net

Note From The Author:

This small book is unique.

It is in some ways a collection of essays.

Eleven men take up words and paint a picture they see
in their memory of a great man.

Nine men called him pastor, two were born out of due season.

This book is written in honor of the 75th Anniversary
of the church he pioneered.

It is written from the vantage point of the years I was in Bakersfield.

There are many other men who have been produced by his ministry.
The writers of this manuscript are the men who impacted me
and were my peers while I was in Bakersfield.

Therefore, it is not a comprehensive picture of the man I. H. Terry.
Herein are vignettes of pieces and periods of his life.

These brief palimpsests reflect the 1970's and early 1980's when
I. H. Terry was in the last decade of his active office as Pastor
of First Pentecostal Church.

Each man wrote as he saw it. It is their view,
their memory, their montage.

Surprisingly there was little repetition. Frankly, I expected more.
As a bouquet of flowers is most brilliant when the colors contrast,
so these men bring pungency and diversity.

The chapters were not edited except for spelling and punctuation. These
pages are their words, their thoughts, their reminisces.

Each man knew I. H. Terry personally.

Each man will attest his life was impacted
by this church pioneer from West Texas.

This edition is dedicated to First Pentecostal Church
of Greater Bakersfield.

It is in honor of I. H. Terry: Our pastor.

It is his legend and his legacy in part.

Kenneth Bow
November, 2018

Table of Contents

Author's Note

Exordium by Larry Booker 1

Chapter 1 — Leon Frost 5

Chapter 2 — Ray Brown 12

Chapter 3 — Robert Condren 18

Chapter 4 — Ron Lawrence 22

Chapter 5 — Johnny King 33

Chapter 6 — Kenneth Bow 42

Chapter 7 — Robert Dansby 59

Chapter 8 — Keith McCoy 66

Chapter 9 — Henry Buczynski 71

Envoi — by Vaughn Morton 74

Exordium

by
Larry Booker

The following chapters you are about to read were written by Pastors who were allowed to be under the ministry and instruction of Rev. Isaac Hilliard Terry. You are about to read funny, powerful, sometimes sad, but always fascinating stories. The life of I.H. Terry was a vast host of uniquely played out and attention-grabbing experiences. If you were allowed to be involved in even one of those experiences, you never forgot it.

In my over 45 years of ministry I have had the opportunity to meet some of the Kingdom's greatest, most remarkable people. While many of these have played indispensable roles in my spiritual formation, Rev. Isaac Hilliard Terry is entrenched in my short list of those who most profoundly affected my life and ministry.

I will never forget pulling our old and somewhat dilapidated travel trailer through the Great American Desert on our way to California in the fall of 1981. Our original plans were to, hopefully, preach in California for three months. During the long drive, I remember my wife and I discussing that during our stay we hoped we could possibly just meet three people that we'd heard so much about; Paul Price, Vaughn Morton and I.H. Terry. Never did we dream that almost forty years later we would still be in

California and that those three men would be among our closest friends and have impacting influences on ours, and our children's, lives.

Though I was not from under Bro. Terry's ministry, I was one of the fortunate's in that he somewhat 'adopted' me by taking me under his fascinating wing. Through the years there were times that Bro. Terry made me mad, frustrated me, hurt my feelings, and made me laugh so hard my sides would ache. He would tell me stories about his life that would literally make me weep. But never one time did I contemplate distancing myself from Rev. I.H. Terry. I was drawn to him like a moth to a light and I loved him very, very much. I am now going to relate the moment that Brother Terry won my heart forever.

The year was 1982 and my family and I attended the U.P.C.I. general conference being held in Salt Lake City. I had met Brother Terry briefly while parking my trailer on the parking lot of the First Pentecostal Church of Bakersfield California, which he had pastored, at that time, for almost 40 years. A friend of mine, Randy Kendrick, excitedly came to me and said Brother Terry wanted to see me, as he had listened to a message that I had preached about Israel – eight times while traveling from Bakersfield to Salt Lake, and that he had also played the tape to the Bakersfield church.

Brother Kendrick took me to a group of about 10 to 12 preachers where Brother Terry was, as was his custom, seated in the midst of them "holding court." As I approached, Brother Terry scooted away whoever was sitting next to him and commanded me to sit by him. Thus began one of the great friendships of my life. The upshot of that meeting was that, because (he thought) I knew so much about Israel, its regathering and 1948 nationhood, that I needed to at least go to Israel and see it for myself. He also told me that if I would carry his luggage he would take me. I was incredulous, but told him that if he was serious I would be his camel. As I found out in April 1984, he was as good as his word and, with the help of Vaughn Morton who paid my wife's expenses, she and I were able to go to Israel with Brother Terry.

At the General Conference service that night, as we sat together in an extremely full auditorium, I remember standing to my feet, cheering and worshiping God as we listened to a powerful message concerning revival. I then felt a tugging on my coat and turned to look down at Brother Terry.

He was looking up at me with tears streaming down his face, presenting a picture of lost despair. As I fell into my seat I heard him say through his tears; "Help me... you've got to help me..." My mind was immediately lost to the service and totally focused on this man, this icon of Pentecost. Leaning in close I whispered; "What's wrong Brother Terry?" "You've got to help me... I need help. My wife has been down in a coma for seven years... and I can't even get enough faith to get her out of bed, and that man is down there is preaching about a million soul revival in the Philippines and I can't even get my wife out of bed... you've got to help me..." To say that my heart broke for this man is an massive understatement. It was also the moment where Rev. I.H. Terry won my heart forever.

From that single incident, it did not matter what Brother Terry ever said or did to me, be it good or bad, honor or rebuke, whether he was happy with me or extremely displeased – he had won me unfailingly to him. I had witnessed another side to the man who was commonly known for his tough, gruff ways, his plainness of speech, great boldness, and uncompromising strength. I witnessed a sorrow and sense of hopelessness that his dear wife's long season of physical trauma had wreaked upon him...and I never, ever forgot it. I was won completely.

Through the years, I have compiled an extensive list of saints and preachers that I have personally known that have passed on into God's glorious eternal reward. Of them all, there are three People that I miss the most, and that very deeply. One of the three is I.H. Terry.

I am sure that since he has arrived, Heaven has become a much more interesting place. If you did not happen to know him personally, you are about to find out as you read this book (at least a little bit) how interesting he really was.

Larry L. Booker
June 25, 2018

Chapter 1

Leon Frost

The legend of I.H. Terry has been repeated often and sometimes it has been misrepresented. The legacy of I.H. Terry lives on in the lives of the men he mentored and guided in the ministry. I am one who is a recipient of his legacy. As I write this portion of the book I am very grateful that Kenneth Bow has considered putting this book together, and is making it available.

There is a portion of the legacy of I.H. Terry already written by and for him that I will try not to duplicate.

His name was Isaac Hillard Terry.

I first met I.H. Terry in 1949. I was only 4 at the time. The church was on 34th Street. This building still stands today. My memories of Dallas Mefford and Sam White and others of that era are still fresh in my mind.

Growing up under the ministry and influence of I.H. Terry has played a major part in the development of my doctrinal beliefs. The impact that he had on my life is why I am in the ministry today. I will forever be grateful for the times we spent together.

Our church has always been a worshipping church. One of my first memories of our church services was in the early 50s. It was a funeral service of a great man that had gone on to meet the Lord. He was the husband of a great worshipping wife, we called her respectfully Granny Watkins. She knew how to worship. At her husband's funeral, she worshipped God in a very powerful way that I have never forgotten. One day she fell asleep while Bro. Terry was preaching. As was the case with Bro. Terry, at times, he would stress in the mike, "Eat it saints." He was referring to the Word of God that he was preaching. This statement was often a part of his message. While he was preaching one night, he said it so forceful that Sister Watkins came out of her sleep with a shout of victory and speaking in tongues, instant in prayer.

Many were the times that Bro. Terry would ring the bell that was on the pulpit to stop the worship so he could preach. One time when Alvin Wilson and I were with him in South America, he sat Molly Thompson, the missionary's wife that was interpreting for him, down because she would not stop worshipping while he was preaching. He definitely was a Word preacher.

I received the Holy Ghost as a young boy. I was 7 years old. Brother Lee was the evangelist. The year was 1953. That was 65 years ago as of this writing. It has been a wonderful time living for God. All those years under the ministry of Brother Terry has given me some great experiences.

The following story speaks of the humility, sincerity and devotion to God that often is over looked when they speak of his hardness or strictness.

Brother Terry and I had attended the funeral of a pastor friend. I was driving his nice green Cadillac. As we were traveling, I thought it would be a good time to open the discussion of my development in the ministry. He was reading the newspaper and not saying anything to me, so I said to him, "Brother Terry, I hope the Lord makes a preacher out of me." He folded the newspaper at the top and looked at me and soberly said, "I hope He makes a Christian out of me." So that ended my desire for discussion about my ministry for a while, while I contemplated being a Christian first.

It was 1971 when Brother Terry told me that he wanted me to stay with him and take the church when he retired.

I had a butcher shop close to the church. Several men became meat cutters after working for me. One who is also in this book was Bob Dansby. Another was David Webb. Brother Terry would come in to buy meat and would visit with me. I guess he thought I could handle money well, so he said, "I need someone who will take care of the church I built."

I do not want to come across as boastful or arrogant, but I will speak to the time and experience of becoming pastor of this great church.

One night after church I was talking with him at the pulpit, he turned to me and pulled out a six-inch knife. You never knew what would be next with Brother Terry, so I watched with carefulness as he opened the blade and handed it to me. He then turned his back on me and said, "Do you know what this means?" I said, "Tell me." He said, "I am going to start preaching you on Sunday nights, don't stab me in the back. Be ready whenever I need you."

I sat next to him on the platform. Many were the Sunday nights that as he was getting up to take the offering he would turn to me and say, "You are running in a few minutes." That meant that I better be ready to preach at a moment's notice. Since he was a doctrinal preacher, it brought new meaning to the scripture, "being instant in season and out of season." I was afraid that the other part of the scripture would suddenly come to his mind if I refused to preach, which says, "reprove and exhort with (well it might not have been) all longsuffering."

Brother Terry did not finish high school, but he was very intelligent. He knew how and when to use help for his illustrations. He was preaching one night on "in the mouth of two or three witnesses let every word be established." He had given the scripture to another man on the platform, 2 Corinthians 13:1. He told me to read Genesis 31:44 *Now therefore come thou, let us make a covenant, I and thou; and let it be for a witness between me and thee.*

Verse 46 *And Jacob said, this unto his brethren, gather stones and they took stones and made a heap; and they did eat there upon the heap. 47. And Laban called it Jegar-Sahadutha...* I had never pronounced that word before, I just read over it. He made me get it right before he went on preaching. I have never forgotten how to pronounce that word to this day. He went on preaching Jesus' name baptism with a heap of witnesses.

You always had to be ready to read for him during his messages. He was a great illustrator. Brother Terry would act out many of his messages with help from his young preachers.

Brother Terry said he only had five messages. Of course, he spoke of the main themes of the gospel. This was not completely true. He was also good at doing the work of an evangelist.

Many of you have heard messages like, "The Author," or "Sign My Note," or "God is not Ashamed to be Called Your God."

The other day, I was looking through some of the notes that I took during his messages. He would start with one scripture and end with another. Then on another occasion he would preach a different message with the same scriptures, only this time he would start from the bottom and go up. He was a very unique preacher.

Brother Terry asked me to sell my business and come to work for him. I sold my business December 31, 1974 and came to work for him January 1, 1975. My pay was $700 a month before taxes. I was the first full time assistant to Brother Terry. I count that a great honor. Others assisted Brother Terry and were also employed.

That first Saturday morning we went to breakfast together. He said, "We will do this every Saturday morning so we can discuss what needs to be done or what has to be done." That was the last Saturday, or any other time that we went to eat together. I guess we got it all figured out in that one breakfast.

During the first couple of years I became more of a fund raiser for the church. We sold cherries, fireworks, and of course Christmas trees. With some of these monies we were able to build the second building on the school property.

Sister Margaret Terry had a stroke on December 15, 1975. That changed my life and certainly it changed Brother Terry's.

Brother Terry was a very devoted husband and companion. He would come home from church or church activities and his first stop before anything else was to check on Sister Terry. He would love on her and pat her like she would be able to respond, but could not because of the deep coma she was in. He would tell her of the problems of the church and tell her to pray. It was known by all that Sister Terry was a prayer warrior. She was also a worshipper. I will never forget hearing her pray and worship.

Prior to and during this time, I was one of the Terry-ite boys. The men in this book were all friends of mine. I am sure you will read of their experiences with Brother Terry. He made you feel like you were a part of him while you were with him. He made each one of his "boys" feel like they were special and have different stories to tell.

During the time after Sister Terry's stroke and time of laying in a coma, I would go to the hospitals to pray for the sick. It was during this time Brother Terry was not comfortable going to the hospital because Sister Terry was at home from the stroke.

Since I was the one going to the hospital, several saints before they passed away had asked me to preach their funeral. I always said, "I will do what Brother Terry wants me to do." It is times like this that your loyalty and integrity better be to the pastor. On one occasion I had been at the side of a dear saint of God when the Lord came for him. We were at the hospital until about two in the morning. On the way out of the hospital a son of his turned to me and said, "You know Dad always wanted you to preach his funeral." I said, "I will do whatever Brother Terry wants me to do." Brother Terry was out of town and in those days we did not have cell phones and I did not know where he was. I knew that his family was loyal to Brother Terry and that they would talk to him as soon as they could. Well, that was on a Tuesday night and Brother Terry was not back until just before service on Thursday night. I did not have a chance to talk with him before service. Evidently the family had not talked with him either. I did not know that they had not talked to Brother Terry and had made the arrangements for service. He did not announce the funeral, so I went to the pulpit to remind Brother Terry that the funeral was Friday at 1p.m. He turned to the audience and said, "That funeral will be at 1 p.m. Friday. He turned back to me and said, "What funeral?" I knew I was in trouble. I said the man's name. He said, "That will never happen again." I knew that the plans for Brother Terry's retirement were put on hold and that I needed to look for a place for my future.

I knew if I stayed loyal to Brother Terry (of course there was never a question whether I would or not) I would need to leave before people would try to put a wedge between us.

I became pastor in Avondale, Arizona in 1978. Brother Terry never came to preach for me while I was there. Three weeks after I came back to Bakersfield, he went to preach for Ray Brown who took my church in Avondale. I would talk with Brother Terry on occasion, but there were times I did not know if I would ever return to Bakersfield.

One Sunday morning about 5:55 a.m. I was awakened by a dream. There are only two dreams in my life that I feel had some significance. This was one of them. I could see two well known men who were members of the First Pentecostal Church. They were standing by the south entrance to the auditorium. One said it will be all right and the other one just waved and walked out. I was talking with Brother Terry and he said, "When I walk away from the pulpit and sit down on the front pew, it will be all yours. I will no longer be pastor." I was so startled by the dream when I woke up that I prayed and said, "God, if there is anything to this dream, I need to know if I am going back to sleep." At 6 a.m. sharp Brother Terry called and said, "I need you to come home." I said, "I can come in two weeks and I will meet you at the Santa Maria camp." When I arrived at the campgrounds, Brother Terry had already left to go home.

Saturday morning I met Brother Terry at the school property for a well-remembered trip on Round Mountain Road. We talked about a lot of different subjects but nothing to do with me coming back home.

When we arrived back at the school property, I said, "You called the other day." That was all I got out of my mouth when he replied, "that was the other day," and put the truck in gear as to go—I knew it was time for me to get out of the truck. Our conversation was over. The dream must have just been another dream.

That was just one of the reasons I thought I probably would not be the next pastor in Bakersfield.

Brother Ewing preached the 40th anniversary and retirement service for

Brother Terry. That night the dream I had some months prior, came true just as I had seen it.

My relationship with Brother Terry became stronger than ever after he became pastor emeritus. He preached in many churches and was able to travel for several years.

Four years before he went to be with the Lord, he came to me and said, "Cut my pay in half the Lord is not happy with me taking this much money." Has any retired preacher ever been that gracious?

Brother Terry was with me for twenty-one years. It was a great journey.

Chapter 2

Ray Brown

The problem facing any biographer of great men is, do you stand up close, or far away? Do you show all the warts or do you focus only on the greatness? In the case of Bro. Terry it is impossible to separate the two. What most men would see as a flaw of character is in fact the source of his greatness. Bro. Terry was not like other men. This is not the story of an ordinary man.

I was born into the Bakersfield church in June of 1947. My mother was expecting me when she started attending Bro. Terry's church. In fact, she started attending because of my sister and myself. She felt she had a responsibility to her children to raise them in church. Thank God for good mothers.

Bro. Terry had moved from West Texas and started the church only a few years before. He came from a wealthy, highly educated family in Stanford, Texas. I met several of his brothers and sisters and all were successful in life. One was a doctor, another a business owner, two were educators, all were successful people. Bro. Terry was the black sheep of the family, a high school dropout. His father was the superintendent of education with a dropout for a son.

He married young and had a son and daughter when his wife left him for another man. He later married the woman we knew as Sis. Terry. While working at an oil supply store in Monahans, Texas, he was invited to church and soon was converted. He felt the call to the ministry and as a local preacher started preaching. Soon he felt the call to go to Bakersfield and start a church.

Bakersfield had been the dust bowl terminus for many dispossessed during the great depression and was filled with former inhabitants of Oklahoma, Arkansas and Texas. Thus, Bro. Terry was trying to start a church in a town filled with people only recently removed from the Bible belt.

He never had a malleable character. One of his great strengths was an unbendable view of the gospel. He demonstrated that view by placing a sign by the front door of his church that read "All Trinitarians are going to Hell." One would think that a man trying to start a new church would not want to alienate any potential visitors, but as I said, he was not like other men.

The first pulpit was two orange crates stacked atop one another. The first song book was mimeographed papers made in the back of the church. Other pastors in the neighborhood predicted he would never build a church but soon the church began to grow.

My earliest memory of the church was on 34th street. It was there he preached his famous "Slinging Mud" sermon. He was preaching against gossip and likened gossip to slinging mud. To demonstrate what he was preaching he brought a bucket of mud to church. While preaching he would quote a gossip and sling mud on the church walls. When we left that church for a new building several years later there were still mud stains on the walls.

We soon moved to 36th and O, a much larger church which was the church I was raised in. In 1967 that church was remodeled and made much larger. Then the present location was built under Bro. Frost. It seats around 900.

For reasons not altogether clear, Bro. Terry had the ability to instill a desire to preach in the men that attended his church. Within a few years of the start of the church young preachers started leaving Bakersfield to start their own churches. Dutchie Clayton, then Sam White, H. K. Duke and others started leaving Bakersfield in a seemingly endless stream of preachers. How did he do it? Good question. First of all, he exuded certainty. If Bro. Terry ever had any doubts of the validity of his doctrine it was never apparent to me.

He was absolute and that certainty seemed to bleed over into the young men that sat at his feet. Robert Browning once said that you can measure a mind's height by the shade it casts, and this was never more true than with Bro. Terry. With only a couple of exceptions all the men that left the Bakersfield church have stayed true to the doctrine taught by Bro. Terry. Considering there is probably upwards of fifty that were taught by Bro. Terry that is an amazing statistic. After all, Jesus hand picked twelve and one of them went bad.

Bro. Terry cast a wide net. He would go to almost every man in the church and encourage him to be open to the ministry. He would encourage men to sit on the platform, as a sign of that openness. He would see potential in men nobody else saw. My brother in law was shy almost beyond description. When he would sing a special he would never raise his eyes to the congregation. Bro. Terry encouraged him to sit on the platform. His first sermons during young people service were painful to watch. He was terrorized. He now pastors a good church in Dallas, Texas. I have no doubt only Bro. Terry could have unlocked the potential in Robert Condren.

At that time we had a large church. There were a lot of men sitting on the platform. When I left for bible school (forgive me, Jesus) there were probably forty men sitting on the platform. Did all enter the ministry? No, not all, but several did.

In the twenty or so years I spent in the Bakersfield church Bro. Terry seemed to take a special interest in me. I got to drive him on several long trips so I probably knew him about as well as any. I have heard stories about Bro. Terry all over Apostolic Pentecost. Just a few weeks ago I received a text asking me if Bro. Terry had a problem smoking cigars? No he did not smoke cigars. Then I heard this one several times. Bro. Terry was sleeping in the back of his truck with Sis. Terry driving when she had to make a sudden stop. Bro. Terry, thinking she had been in a wreck, jumped out of the truck only to have Sis. Terry drive away with Bro. Terry chasing her down the road. Sorry, brethren, it didn't happen.

Now let me tell you one that did. Bro. Terry was the child of a different technological age. Once he was fitted for a lapel mic. Not being used to a lapel mic is dangerous. After having the mike attached to his coat, and not being aware it was on, Bro. Terry made preparation to go on the platform to start the service. He went to his office bathroom and noisily used the toilet. Then he cleared his throat right into the mic. Then he rid himself of unwanted intestinal gas, thinking better here in the bathroom rather than on the platform. Then, finally ready for church he left his office and walked on to the platform and wondered why the whole congregation was rolling on the floor. My source for this story? Bro. Terry himself. And he wasn't laughing.

Bro. Terry was the most eccentric man I have ever had close dealings with. Every time I had a conversation with Bro. Terry he would say something I would not understand. When I would ask for an explanation of his statement he would explain, but I wouldn't understand that either. A great Greek philosopher once said that the road up and the road down was the same road. I think the secret to his greatest successes came from his deep eccentricity.

Honesty demands that I state that there were a lot of people that did not care for Bro. Terry. He was easily misunderstood and there were times when he was completely understood, and both could cause him trouble.

As a child I remember sitting in service when about forty people got up and walked out, never to return. He was voted in as sectional presbyter one time and at the next election he got one vote. He was not easy to live with, but then he could do the kindest things. I have been asked many times if I thought Bro. Terry could build a church today using his methods. The answer is yes.

I evangelized for fifteen years and on numerous occasions Bro. Terry would see me somewhere and hand me a $100.00 bill. And that was when $100.00 was a week's pay. We had a very dysfunctional family in our church with a boy about twelve years old. The boy was big and beefy and a bully and was not popular. Bro. Terry took him a bicycle for his birthday when his own family got him nothing.

In his later years this same eccentricity exhibited itself in his selection of sermons to preach. Many questioned the propriety of his sermons and I hated that he would go all over the country preaching things that would taint his memory, but I was not the one to straighten him out. He was my pastor. It was not my job to correct him. The last time he preached for me someone had brought up a controversial subject and his answer included a word not normally acceptable in Apostolic Pentecost, but I said nothing. His greatest strength and his greatest weakness sprang from the same source.

Bro. Terry associated with a group of men that back in the 1960s left the UPCI for other organizational affiliations. Bro. Terry was invited to join them but he went the other way and became a champion of the UPCI. This was considered a strange move for a man who only a few years before had been the victim of an attempt to get him out of the organization. The district superintendent of California had plotted with the general superintendent in St. Louis to get Bro. Terry out. The plot failed when the district superintendent of California got voted out of office. How do I know all this? The general superintendent of the UPCI, Bro. A.T. Morgan, came by Bakersfield and apologized to Bro. Terry in front of the whole congregation for allowing himself to be involved in such a plot. So when Bro. Terry began to beat the drum in favor of the UPCI it seemed strange to most of the Bakersfield boys.

It is in the nature of most great men to want subservience from those around them. Bro. Terry definitely wanted his boys to follow his lead in our relationship with the UPCI. Soon, however, Bro. Mefford left and in 1997 I followed in my departure from the organization. My decision was based on what I saw as the deteriorating condition of the organization in Arizona. I did not want my church to be tainted with the fellowship of people who did not want old fashioned Pentecost. I went to Bro. Terry and tried to explain my motives for leaving the mothership but to his dying day he resented my leaving what he was espousing.

Bro. Terry supported the UPCI for reasons that were not held by the vast majority. Deep in the core of Bro. Terry's eccentricity was idealism. He saw the organization as this perfect vehicle to support foreign missions. He would preach we have to bring the King back. So support of foreign missions was the driving force behind his campaign to keep his boys in the UPCI. Not being blessed with the idealism that fueled Bro. Terry's world view, I saw things a little differently. The purpose of this book is not to give me a platform to preach my view point so I will spare you, but to say that Bro. Terry did not agree with me would be a vast understatement. He openly rebuked me on a couple of occasions until I got a chance to explain my world view to Bro. Terry. Until the day he died he would bring up my leaving the organization as a disappointment to him. I think he began to accept the inevitable when almost all his men left the organization. So strong was his influence that several waited to leave the UPCI until he died. Free Pentecost was a nasty word in the Bakersfield church and Bro. Terry was afraid that without the organization we would become free Pentecost. I was more afraid of carnal Pentecost than free Pentecost.

Bro. Terry gave away hundreds of knives in his lifetime and many bibles. Bro. Terry was a wealthy man who made several wise financial decisions in his lifetime, but nevertheless he would go to the county dump almost every day. He collected antiques and knives and it was impossible to best Bro. Terry in a trade. Bro. Ken Bow has several of Bro. Terry's bibles and I have none. The bible says if you have ought of this world's goods and see your brother in need and shut up the bowels of compassion how dwelleth the love of God in you?

Like so many today who live to an advanced old age he outlived his health. Even the men who were raised by Bro. Terry began to die. He began to visibly fail the last couple of years of his life, and it was interesting to see the preachers trooping to his door to see him for the last time, including me. I made it a point to see him often. It has been said that great men are not accounted as great in their own generation but that didn't work with Bro. Terry. Many thought we were seeing the passing of an Apostle and I am not sure they were wrong.

I have also read that when judging great men you cannot take into account their small faults. It would be easy to find fault with so different a man but that is not in my heart today. I only remember the greatness that brought me the gospel and helped to keep California strong for a generation.

My entire life has been lived in the shadow of Bro. Terry. I rejoice in that shadow. I feel safe knowing I am continuing in the Apostle's Doctrine that was taught me as a child. I have been asked by many men what it is like to be from Brother Terry's church and to be one of the preachers he turned out. It is truly like belonging to an exclusive club whose membership is now closed forever.

Rest in peace Bro. Terry, I will be along in a few days.

Chapter 3

Robert Condren

I first met Bro. Terry in 1953, at the little church on 1000 34th St. in Bakersfield, Ca. I was 12 years old and Bro. Terry was 41 years old. Our whole family of 5 came in, got the Holy Ghost and got baptized during a revival with Bro. Sandberg.

The new church at 1001 36th St. was being completed and we moved over in April of 1954.

Bro. Terry would buy old roll up window shades at thrift stores and use them to put his scriptures on for his One God, New Birth messages. He made it so plain.

Bro. Terry, when he wanted to make a point would rub his whiskers on the microphone for emphasis.

When other preachers were preaching, and Bro. Terry liked the point he was making, he'd tell the church, "Eat it saints."

Bro. Terry was a great mentor of young preachers. He unselfishly sent men out when he thought they were ready. A few "just went" and were not successful. He was a good judge of character and knowledge of the Word. In 1961 Bro. Verbal Bean came to our church and added a new dimension. My wife and I got married the first Friday night of the revival and the revival continued about 10 weeks, which was a very long revival in those days, with church every night and prayer meeting every morning. That revival was a wonderful, life changing revival for the Bakersfield Church. About 100 people got the Holy Ghost but lots were from out of town that had come to visit the revival, and we never saw them again, but the residual of that revival is still with us today.

As Bro. Terry started to use me, he put me in charge of service one night while the more experienced "helps" were working on the church expansion, next door. We had Bro. Cranford visiting and Bro. Terry was checking out the progress next door, during church. After song service, in my inexperience, I just put Bro. Cranford on the floor. About that time Bro. Terry came back in and got mad because the preacher was on the floor and he sat him down and had me have some testimonies and prayer requests, which I had forgotten to do in my nervousness. A good lesson learned that I never forgot.

Bro. Terry had a "system" that worked for many years with his young preachers. He would have you sit on the platform to start "grooming" you to be used. The chair closest to him was his assistant, the next chair was service leader or song leader, down farther was Youth Leader and so on.

As men would leave to go preach, Bro. Terry assigned the next chair you sat in. One funny occasion happened to my brother-in-law, Bro. Ray Brown. Someone had just left to go preach and Bro. Brown was one of the younger men on the platform, but Bro. Terry decided he wanted him to sit in the vacated chair. One of the older men noticed he'd put his Bible under the chair before church and suggested that an older man should have that chair. Bro. Brown didn't tell him Bro. Terry told him to sit there, he just said well, you're right and moved down to another chair. When Bro. Terry came in, he said, "I thought I told you to sit in that chair," Bro. Brown said, "This brother told me not to," and he had Bro. Brown go ahead and sit there and told the older brother to "come with him," and they had a little conversation and that was the end of that. Bro. Terry ruled his platform.

Bro. Terry was a Word preacher. When he would be preaching to reach a sinner with the Gospel, he would walk the aisles so anointed, preaching the Plan of Salvation and it was thrilling. Anytime I would visit him after we left for the ministry, we would discuss the Bible and he'd have several Bibles around and you never left without him reading and answering questions right out of the Bible.

One time, he was so excited that God had shown him something to "stop the mouths of the gainsayers." One of the men that had left to go preach was leaving the principles of the doctrine and saying all we need to do is "abstain from meats offered to idols, and from blood and from things strangled and from fornication." God enlightened Bro. Terry with I Cor. 4:17, that Paul preached (his doctrine) everywhere, in every church. He was so excited, and it was exciting to me.

Bro. Terry recounted a funny incident in his younger ministry. They had an evangelist and times were poor, no money for a motel, and they only had 1 bedroom and 1 bed. Nothing to do but share their bed, a regular size bed, I might add, so the evangelist slept on one side with Bro. Terry in the middle with Sis Terry on the other side.

Another funny incident happened to us. We had invited Bro. and Sis Terry over for dinner and to talk and ask advice. We only lived 3 houses down from my in-laws, so we told our kids to go down there until after we ate so we could visit. Well, our oldest son told our middle son (about 4-5) to come see what's going on. So, he walked in and stood around and Bro. Terry didn't want him to hear us discussing things, so he reached up and thumped him on the head good and he ran down to Grandma's house crying. We just laughed about it. I don't think Grandma was happy about it but of course she didn't say anything, except to us.

In 1969 our church won the Sheaves for Christ award for most money raised that year. My wife and I were the head of that endeavor. We raised $22,222.22. That was Bro. Terry. He wanted us to go to General Conference that year to accept the award with him. So, I bought a new suit, tie, shoes and was so excited to go to our first conference. Bro. Terry got the bright idea of renting head gear and a mesh armor. He wore the armor and I got to wear the head gear. It was hot and sweaty, plastered my hair to my head, and I had to take it off with these thousands of people looking on. He used the scripture, I Kings 20:11 "not him that girdeth on his harness boast himself, as he that taketh it off." It was typical Bro. Terry.

Some relatives tried to entice us away from Bakersfield by telling my wife she could play the piano for their choir, we could sing and be used. We went to Bro. Terry to ask his advice and he said "no" and that was the end of that. We didn't question, we listened and we're so thankful that we did.

I was so backward I couldn't hardly say my name and God had been dealing with me about the ministry. One night during testimony service I dutifully stood to testify but that night God loosed my tongue and anointed me and the whole church knew God had done a marvelous thing.

I was the Youth Leader for 5 years. Bro. Terry left me in charge of our church at times and one time I got to baptize a boy that had gotten the Holy Ghost. God began to use me, and I guess Bro. Terry took notice so in 1971, one night after church, Bro. Terry came and told me that he wanted me to go to Roseville, CA. Bro. Stevens had started that church and wanted to come back home and Bro. Terry said we were ready. I told my wife and we started selling our home, packing up and never looked back. We never questioned his wisdom. We were in Roseville 2 ½ yrs. and felt God leading us to the evangelistic field. We went for counsel to one of the men out of our church who lived nearby, and he told us we could make it on the field if we'd leave Bro. Terry's doctrine, but we might lose our kids. He was wrong on both counts. God blessed us on the field, but before we left Bro. Terry said we'd probably go places that had rings, women wore pants and cut their hair. Such was the climate in UPC even back then.

While we were evangelizing Bro. Mefford encouraged us to leave UPC and join AMF. We did, and it caused a lot of turmoil with Bro. Terry. When we would come home, Bro. Terry wouldn't recognize me but allowed my wife to sing and testify. He did soften his stance on it though and came to preach for us in Dallas around 1995. We were struggling about whether to build a new church. We didn't want to get in a mess financially. He asked how much we were looking to spend and Bro. Steve Coon had looked at our plans and estimated about $150,000. We only had about 40 people. He said, "go ahead and build it, that's just the price of a house," so we went into the building program feeling reassured with his blessings.

Bro. Terry will always be highly esteemed in my eyes for what he put in my heart. A wonderful foundation of Truth that I'm able to pass on to the next generation.

Chapter 4

Ron Lawrence

My pathway to and memories of the man who would impact and change my life more than any other man: my Pastor Bro I. H. Terry.

My eighth grade and half of my freshman year was at Hayward, California where myself, my Dad, my older brother Melton and my younger brother Jim received the Holy Ghost under Bro. Edgar. The second half of my freshman year was at Phoenix Union High in Phoenix, Arizona.

For my sophomore year our family had settled in Fresno, CA, where we attended Bro. Earl Tool's church. When Bro. Verbal Bean started a revival at Bro. Murray Lane's church we went on our church's off nights as often as possible.

An interesting bit of history of the Fresno church that involved my dad; one day Bro. Murray Lane, Bro. Verbal Bean, and Bro. Bill Garrett came by my parents upholstery shop and picked up my dad so that he could inspect a bus they wanted to buy and use for Sunday School. It was Fresno's first bus. Bro. Garrett traded his family car for it—or sold his car and bought it.

It was 1961—I had just completed my sophomore year at Roosevelt High School in Fresno, California, and the Lawrence's were getting ready to move again.

This time we were moving to Bakersfield, CA, and with relatives in Bro. Leon Stobaugh's church in Bakersfield and Bro. Paul Winters church in Lamont, it was God and Bro. Verbal Bean's 13-week revival that convinced my parents to become members of Bro. Terry's church. Their motto at that time was, "36th and O, the best place to go."

It was during our 13 week revival with Bro. Bean in the Bakersfield church that Bro. Bean's vision and faith for a 100 soul revival came to pass.

I was just a 16 year old boy at the time, but looking back on that revival, I can see how Bro. Terry and Bro. Bean complemented each other's ministry. Bro. Terry was the best doctrinal preacher I've ever met and and Bro. Bean was the best preacher I've ever met at contending for and getting a move of the Holy Ghost.

In regards to Bro. Terry being a doctrinal. Preacher— as I write this chapter, it was 57 years ago that I met Bro. Terry and he became my pastor. Now that I have pastored for 40 years, I continue to preach and believe the doctrines I learned from Bro. Terry.

Brother Terry was one of a kind and those who tried to clone him failed and those who were challenged by him succeeded.

The Bro. Terry we met when we moved to Bakersfield was the one who claimed that at this time in his ministry, that if he heard something about you, the knock on your door at 2 AM could be Bro. Terry wanting to talk about the problem.

Understanding that trait of Bro. Terry, it was during Bro. Bean's revival, and we had only been going to Bro. Terry's church for 3 or 4 weeks, when there was a knock on our door. When we opened the door it was Bro. Terry and Bro. Bean standing there. Bro. Terry had come to talk to my mom and dad about their tithes and offerings. Being a minister now I can only imagine how Bro. Bean felt when Bro. Terry said, "Bro. Bean come go with me. I need to talk to a new family about their tithes and offerings." Those who knew Bro. Terry know that when he said come go with me you just went without questioning. That was my family's personal introduction to the man we would proudly call our pastor.

Bro. Terry absolutely loved this one God, Jesus Name, apostolic holiness message.

Bro. Terry was a major driving force in the California district of the UPCI. He strengthened the preachers of his, and my, generation as to the absolute essentiality of being baptized in Jesus Name according to Acts 2:38, and that we had to believe in One God to be saved and that Jesus was that one God manifest in the flesh (2 Corinthians 5:19, Ephesians 4:5, James 2:19). Bakersfield was blessed by having Bro. Terry for our pastor and by having the best preachers in Pentecost preach for us. One of the things he taught his young men was that you didn't have to be the best preacher, you could get good preachers to come preach for you, but you did have to be a good steward of God's work.

I'll never forget blind Bro. Joe Duke who was the next evangelist after Bro. Bean. He claimed that he could see more with his spiritual eyes that we could see with our natural eyes. I can't remember how many nights it took, but Bro. Terry had the entire church line up at his office door and individually walk into the office where Bro. Terry and Bro. Joe Duke were standing on the other side of a counter. Bro. Joe Duke would take our hand and tell us what the spirit showed him about our lives. Trust me, we were all sweating bullets.

I remember Bro. Terry going to the meeting where they started the AMF fellowship. Many of the founding preachers were personal friends with Bro. Terry and were expecting him to join them as the west coast representative for the AMF. Many of the preachers in California were waiting on Bro. Terry to make a decision and if he went with the AMF they were going also. Bro. Terry decided not to join the AMF instead he came home and preached a sermon he titled "Flying United." This was his way of saying that he was not joining the AMF but was staying with the UPC. Some were disappointed that he didn't join this new fellowship because all of the major preachers in the AMF had preached for us in Bakersfield and had been an influence in our lives. To this day some believe he made the right decision others believe he didn't.

Bro. Terry took everything his boys did personal, so when Bro. Dallas Mefford went with the AMF Bro. Terry severed his and our fellowship with Bro. Mefford. The consequence of this decision was that we missed out on

some of the most powerful productive years of Bro. Medford's ministry. I don't know what year it was but Bro. Terry did reconnect with Bro. Mefford and today I count Bro. Mefford my dearest and most cherished Elder.
Let me reminisce with you over a few of the preachers that came by Bakersfield before I went to Sunnyvale to pastor.

The one who was really good at, and who really loved preaching the oneness of God, was Bro. Howard Boyt. He had so many stories he told about preaching this oneness message at different places. He preached with so much energy and anointing that sweat would drip off him. He would give us verses to read and when you read your verse he would lean over and point to your Bible while sweat dripped off his chin and nose onto your Bible. I don't know where he read it but I remember him quoting what he called the Cotton Patch translation of Colossians 2:9 "For in Him God put all his eggs in one basket."

We had a black preacher from California, somewhere north of Bakersfield, who had preached for us a couple of times when the incident I want to share with you took place. He was good. As he preached he would say, "let me break it down a little finer," then he would. He did that two or three times and every time he would break it down a little finer. One night while he was preaching he said, "It's like when you're sitting there watching Wagon Train and the wagon master says wagons ho and everyone cracks the whip and they all head west together." Every eye in the church snapped toward and fastened on Bro. Terry, and as he had a habit of doing he rubbed his bald head with his right hand. We never saw the preacher again.

We had a young evangelist, who will go unnamed, who preached several times for us. He could hear a sermon one time and preach it almost verbatim only better than the original. You preachers will enjoy this. He assisted Bro. H. K. Duke in Fremont. Bro. Duke had his bags and briefcase packed getting ready to leave for the airport to preach for Bro. O. C. Marler. His assistant said, by the way Bro. Duke you know this sermon you preach I've already preached it there. Bro. Duke said that's ok let's go. His assistant said, "you know this sermon you preach, I've already preached it there," and he went through several of Bro. Duke's best sermons with the same statement. Bro. Duke said, "I'm gonna kill you." Before he flew to Texas Bro. Duke had to go back to his office and get some other sermons.

This same evangelist was good at sports, and loved all sports so much that he went places so he could watch the games on TV. When Bro. Terry heard about what he was doing and he never invited him back. Bro. Terry didn't hide it from his boys; his comment to us was, "he preaches in the attic but he lives in the basement."

Let me set the stage so you get a picture of what was going on. It was the night service after my mother-in-law, Sis. Velda Johnson's funeral earlier that day. Sis. Velda was the sister of Bro. Ray Brown's mother and dearly loved by everyone in church, so we were all grieving. Bro. Terry turned the service over to our guest speaker Bro. Billy Cole. He read his text and made a few comments and then he shut his Bible looked at the church and said, "You don't want to hear what I have to say," and walked out the side door of the church that led to Bro. Terry's office. We all looked at Bro. Terry and he just rubbed his bald head, sent someone out to see if Bro. Cole was coming back. When Bro. Terry learned that he wasn't coming back, Bro. Terry dismissed the church. Just for the record, it probably wasn't right, but all the young men on Bro. Terry's platform looked at each other, shrugged our shoulders, and said, "you know I think he's right."

Since he contributed the envoi in this book, let me say that I was one of Bro. Terry's boys sitting on the platform when Bro. Vaughn R. Morton came to Bakersfield for revival and his introduction to my Pastor, Bro. Terry. Before Bro. Terry invited Bro. Morton to come he called Bro. Price and said if this Morton preacher is any good let's help him, if not let's kill him. Bro. Price said he's a good man. Bro. Terry set out to help him. All I can say is they were both right. Bro. Morton is a good man.

Let me say this for it is connected with Bro. Morton. Bro. Terry gave me a pocket knife when I was a young minister sitting on his platform in Bakersfield and somehow I lost it. I was always asking him for another knife. I hated to grovel but I wanted one of Bro. Terry's knives. I was pastoring and would come home and Bro. Terry would be giving away pocket knives. I would ask him for a knife he would say, did I ever give you one, I would say yes sir. He would just turn and walk off. He was old and retired and giving away all his knives when my wife Alice and I went by to see him. I was determined to get me another knife to replace the one I had lost. I said, Bro. Terry I'm sick of hearing Bro. Morton preach and brag that you have given him 10 knives and he's not even one of your boys.

I don't want to come to your funeral and not have a knife in my pocket that you've given me. I know that was mean, but I was desperate. He said Bro. Lawrence see that cabinet over there, just open that drawer and take any knife you want. I did.

Bro. Terry loved his young men, he called us his boys and he watched over us with a father's love. 1 Corinthians 4:15 *For though ye have ten thousand instructors in Christ, yet have ye not many fathers: for in Christ Jesus I have begotten you through the gospel.* This verse to me describes what Bro. Terry was in my life. The difference between a father and just an instructor is that the father cares more about the results whereas the instructor cares more about the beauty and eloquence of the lesson.

In Bro. Terry's young minister's class our assignment from Bro. Terry would be for us to read one of Paul's letters to Titus or Timothy several times every day preparing us for the next week's class. He would start there but you never knew where he would go. He would talk about the experiences he had with some of the California preachers when he first came to California, naming names. Men who believed it but were weak on the message and how he would use his window shades to preach doctrine at their fellowship meetings. The presbyter would say, "we have about 10 minutes before we eat, we want Bro. Terry to come and say something." He would preach for at least an hour, while the food got cold, and he said that the people there loved to hear him preaching sound doctrine.

He taught us that he really didn't want us to evangelize. His explanation was that he didn't want us to pick cotton and put into someone else's cotton sack but to pick and put it in your own sack. He talked to us about how to pick a city to go to. He said to always pick a city where your young people could grow up, get married and get a job locally. Then he would tell us about a good preacher he knew whose church only had older people on social security because all of the young people had to move to the big city to find work.

He taught us that when your church was small and couldn't support you that you had time to work and then when it grew to the point that it took most of your time that it would be able to support you. Bro. Terry taught us that if you quit too soon you became idle and you would hurt the church and if you worked too long you would neglect and hurt the church. Bro. Terry was always the teacher and he always had some scripture he was considering when he came by he would ask what the verse meant. I believe that he always had the answer before he asked us but he wanted to hear our answer. The one I remember in particular was Ecclesiastes 7:8.

Bro. Terry was a soul winner. We had just finished the expansion of the church on 36th and O when Bro. Terry had an insurance man show up to give him a quote. I was standing in the lobby and heard Bro. Terry say to him "come with me." As we walked through the church Bro. Terry saw a chair in the hallway by the men's restroom. He sat the man down in the chair and asked for my Bible. He had the man read Acts 2:37-38 then said to the man "that's what it takes to be saved."

I can't tell you how many times Bro. Terry drew his mountain with his little stick man on the mountain on the chalk board of our young minister's class and said, "you can go to the top, to the middle or stay at the bottom it's all up to you." In conjunction to his mountain he would challenge us with a stanza from Henry Wadsworth Longfellow's poem, The Ladder of St. Augustine.

> *The heights by great men reached and kept*
> *Were not attained by sudden flight,*
> *But they, while their companions slept,*
> *Were toiling upward in the night.*

I hadn't started preaching yet and was sitting in the congregation on the end of the pew, with my wife, on about the third row. Bro. Terry had left the platform and was walking the aisles of the church preaching and when he came by me he mussed my hair on the side of my head and said, "this is too bushy" and just kept on walking and preaching.

I was 25 when he asked me if I was interested in or felt a calling to preach. I said "yes." He said "get you a coat, a white shirt and a tie and sit on the platform." My first sermon ever was at our Tuesday night youth service. Bro. Terry ran the youth service because it was his training ground for his young ministers. Every young minister who showed up and wanted to, got to preach until the time ran out. Bro. Terry would give everyone a number and then he would have someone call out a number and if it was your number they picked then it was your time to step up and preach.

I'm thinking it was 5 minutes that he gave us and when your time was up he would ring a bell. If he enjoyed what you were saying he would let you go longer, if not he rang the bell. It wasn't long after my first sermon that I got a call from Bro. Terry. All he said was that there's a train going through town on Sunday night and you're on the main line. That was the same message I got every time he asked me to preach after that. Just for the record it was quite a while before he gave me another Sunday night.

In Bakersfield you had to be ready at all times for whatever Bro. Terry wanted you to do. It would be close to service time and Bro. Terry would walk in and as he walked to the platform he would point at one of us men and say you lead service and you lead songs. When Bro. Terry finished his sermon I would pause for a second to see if he had someone scheduled to do his altar song and if nobody moved I stepped to the microphone and did his altar song.

Bro. Terry was totally tone deaf and Sis. Terry couldn't sing. One year they came back from General Conference with a song they wanted the church to learn so Bro. Terry called me up to the pulpit to teach the church a new song that only he and Sis. Terry had ever heard or knew. We somehow got through it and the church sang the song for years. The words were, "He's sweet I know, he's sweet I know, dark clouds may rise and strong winds may blow, but I'll tell the world everywhere I go, that I have found a savior and He's sweet I know."

Alice and I had pastors who wanted us to come assist them, Bro. Croy in Tucson, Arizona, and Bro. C. A. Pricket in Reno, Nevada. When I asked Bro. Terry he said "no." So that option was off the table. When Bro. Alan Abbey in Sacramento asked us to come assist him Bro. Terry said go check it out and if you like it you can go. We went liked it, told the Abbeys we would come and went back to Bakersfield. Bro. Abbey announced to his church that we were coming and everyone was excited.

We came home and invited Bro. and Sis. Terry over for dinner to tell them what we had decided. Bro. Terry grilled us with questions. What is he paying you? Are you both working for him? What is he paying your wife? What are your duties? He said "he's getting two quality people to work for less than he should be paying just you Bro. Ronnie, that's not the will of God." Then Sis. Terry, whom I had never really heard say too much, spoke up and said "that's right, that's not the will of God." The other reasons Bro. Terry gave was that we were too close in age and that if there was ever a problem between Bro. Abbey and myself since he was the pastor I would have a cloud over my head even if I was right. I called Bro. Abbey that night and told him that we weren't coming.

The opportunity to come to the Bay Area came through my good friend Bro. Ken Bow. He was evangelizing at the time when Bro. L. A. McVay asked him if he would consider taking his church. Bro. Bow said "no but I have a friend who might be interested" and gave him my phone number. We came and preached, went home told Bro. Terry about the town and the church, his words were "that's the will of God do it." My first sermon as pastor was January 30, 1977. I still appreciate Bro. Terry's guidance and I am thankful that I listened.

Unless you were one of Bro. Terry's boys you will never understand the connection that we feel toward each other. I have had prominent preachers in our ranks express how lonely and friendless they felt. As one of Bro. Terry's boys I've never felt lonely or friendless. We Bakersfield boys could be apart for a year and when we finally got together again it was like we had just seen each other yesterday.

Allow me to reminisce about a few of Bro. Terry's sermons.

He was great sermon illustrator. For his sermon, "You Paid Too High a Price For Your Whistle," he had a little sliding toy whistle that he would blow as he preached one of his Bible characters. He preached about Adam and every time he would bring up another point he would blow the toy whistle and say, Adam you're paying to high a price for your whistle you're trading your relationship with God for just a little toy whistle. Esau, you paid too high a price for your whistle.

I had him come up and preach to my married couples. He taught his lesson, "Keep the Home Fires Burning," to Sis. Lawrence and I it was just Bro. Terry, for my people they had never heard anything like it in their lives. There were lots of squirming and red faces as he taught.

As I drove him home he asked me if I thought he was independent, I said Bro. Terry you are the most independent preacher I have ever met in my life, nobody's going to tell you what to do. He didn't deny it, he just laughed and smiled.

One night he was preaching a sermon on the Oneness of God with a statue of Buddha off to the side sitting on the edge of the platform. As he preached he walked over to the statue picked up a hammer and started beating the statue to pieces. He stopped, looked at the congregation and said, if you had even a twinge of feelings about this you don't really believe in the oneness of God.

One night he was preaching about Naaman, he was on the platform about two feet away from me when he held his nose and dipped down and counted one, when he dipped down and came up for seventh time I looked at him and the presence of God and the anointing was so powerful that there was a goose bump under every whisker on his face.

Some of my best times with Bro. Terry were sitting around after church and just listening to him talk.

People have said to me that they didn't believe Bro. Terry could build a church today because of his pastoral style. My opinion has always been that Bro. Terry loved the gospel and loved people, and that no matter where you placed him in history he would have built a successful church. He always attracted people no matter where he was. During my 16 years in Bakersfield I saw a Bro. Terry who no longer came to your house at midnight to talk about a problem. He got, and let you get, a good night's sleep and then dealt with it when he saw you next. At one time in his ministry he disfellowshipped every one that backslid and left the church. I remember when one particular man decided to quit living for God and leave the church. He went to Bro. Terry and said, "I'm leaving the church, I'm not going to cause you or the church any problems but if you get up and publicly disfellowship me I will sue you for everything you've got." Bro. Terry didn't and to my knowledge never did it again.

I feel it fitting to close my chapter with the stanza from Longfellow's poem that preceded the one that Bro Terry used to challenge "all his boys!"

> **The distant mountains, that uprear**
> **Their solid bastions to the skies,**
> **Are crossed by pathways, that appear**
> **As we to higher levels rise.**

As I live my life I see the wisdom of the man who was my Pastor, Bro. I. H. Terry. His counsel was from the perspective of seeing the pathways that weren't visible from my position on the mountain: I was still at the bottom and he was at the top.

I've mentioned the great times we have when Bro. Terry's boys get together. Can you imagine what it will be like when we all get together around the throne? I can see it now, people will point and say, "What's going on over there," and someone will say, "Oh, that's just Bro. Terry and his boys having a good time." Do you think God might give him a little bell to quieten us all down so we can all hear him talk?

Just tell them when you saw me I was on my way.

Chapter 5

Johnny King

My pastor, I.H. Terry, was baptized in Jesus' Name by A.H. Browning on February 12, 1939 in Monahans, Texas. He earnestly sought for the Holy Ghost for about a year and a half before receiving it at home in the trailer house they lived in, screaming in tongues and awakening the entire trailer park.

In 1943 he and his wife, Maggie, started the church in Bakersfield, California. He pastored the church for 40 years before retiring at the age of 71. After he "retired" he traveled and preached throughout North America and overseas as long as health permitted.

He baptized me in the wonderful Name of Jesus Christ for the remission of sins when I was a boy. He taught me the truth. His influence in my life is incalculable. I doubt if I would be saved today if not for I.H. Terry.

I.H. Terry was begotten by the Gospel and defined by the Truth. He preached Truth not as an abstract but as an absolute. He loved Truth not as some stubbornly held private principle but as the intimate expression of the Almighty God.

His message was Peter's message. His gospel was Paul's gospel. It was the same old, Apostolic doctrine that began at Jerusalem. He preached it without apology, without hesitation, without equivocation, and without deceit.

There is only One God. That One God was manifest in the flesh. God was in Christ reconciling the world unto Himself. And there was only one way to the One God; repentance, baptism in Jesus' Name for the remission of sins, receiving the Holy Ghost, speaking with other tongues as the Spirit gives the utterance, and living a life of holiness and separation unto the Lord. Peter preached it. Phillip preached it. Paul preached it. "If we, or an angel from heaven preach any other gospel unto you, let him be accursed." (Gal 1.8)

Mom's Memories

My earliest reminisces about Pastor I. H. Terry are not my own but my mother's. Before I was even conceived, my mother's search for God took her to the church in Bakersfield, California pastored by Bro. Terry. It so happened that Bro. Terry taught on tithes that service and got very pointed about who he was preaching to. Brownie Parker knew he was being preached to, got up and slugged Bro. Terry in the jaw. Then he picked up his guitar and was about to slam it down on Bro. Terry's head. Bro. Terry simply lowered his head as if to say, "Go ahead and hit me with your guitar." Brownie resisted the temptation to hit him again, but walked out saying, "The next time I see you, I will kill you." That was Brownie's last time in that church. The foregoing scared my little mama so bad that she jumped up and ran out. She had never seen anything like that in church. She had never heard a man preach as directly as Bro. Terry had. And she probably felt like Brownie Parker was in the right for slugging the pastor. I think she made up her mind that she would never go back to that church. But God wasn't finished with her, and she made it back, received the Holy Ghost, and was attending Bro. Terry's church when I was born.

Object Lessons

She also remembered the time Bro. Terry preached about mud-slinging and demonstrated his message by carrying a bucket of mud through the sanctuary, throwing mud all over the walls, floor and ceiling. I'm sure some of it got on the audience too. When the congregation left that building for a larger facility, there were still mud stains on the ceiling and walls. Bro. Terry commonly illustrated his messages with uncommon object lessons. His object lessons helped the message to "stick" in your mind like the mud stuck to the walls.

He wore a judge's robe and wig when preaching about *The Righteous Judge*. He planted a knife and brass knuckles on a man and "accidentally" discovered them when he preached about *Search Me Oh God and Know My Heart*. He preached *God is Not Ashamed to be Called Their God* in the church I pastored and made me stand in the corner during his entire message but poured the offering into my pockets and added hundreds of dollars from his own pockets at the climax of the message.

Working for Bro. Terry

I went to work for Bro. Terry when I was about 13 years old. He paid me a dollar a day, and usually a Slurpee a day. He owned an antique store called *The Antique Silo*. His profit went to missions. He enjoyed collecting antiques and he enjoyed getting a bargain. He told me, "Don't call me 'Brother Terry or Pastor' when I'm making a bargain." We would drive to yard sales and he would purchase items and have me carry them to his vehicle. He almost always drove a Chevrolet pickup truck in those days. After making the yard sale rounds we might drive to the city dump. He would walk through and point out items for me to put in the truck. On most days we would make a stop at 7-11 where he introduced me to Slurpees. Eventually he would drive back to the shop to clean and display his purchases. If he made an especially good deal he might call Bro. Dick Smith to gloat.

One time I found an old, empty trunk in the garage of the house we lived in across the street from the church. I told Bro. Terry about it and he offered me twenty-five cents for it. On my way back to the church with the trunk, Bro. Smith stopped me and asked me what I was going to do with it. I said I was going to sell it to Bro. Terry for twenty-five cents. Bro. Smith quickly told me he would give me a dollar for it. I sold it to Bro. Smith and then told Bro. Terry what I had done. I could tell he was miffed. He said, "Why honey, I wouldn't walk across the street to see that trunk." Bro. Smith was gloating that day. I went to work for Bro. Smith for fifty cents an hour.

Maggie's Stroke

Although I was traveling as an evangelist at the time, I happened to be in Bakersfield when Sis. Marguerite Terry had the stroke that put her in a coma for seven years until she died. I went to the hospital and was allowed into the Intensive Care Unit. I parted the curtain and stepped into the cubicle where she was being kept. Bro. Terry was sitting by her bedside. There was no one else there. He glanced up at me and, without acknowledging my presence, turned back to what he had been doing. He was talking to his wife. She lay unmoving and unresponsive in the bed, connected by various tubes and wires to drip bags and monitors. There was the periodic beep as her vital signs were being monitored.

Bro. Terry was saying, "I love you. I sure do love you. Do you hear me Maggie? I love you." Of course, there was no response. This went on until I got uncomfortable. I already felt like an intruder. I slipped through the curtains and walked away with my pastor's voice behind me. "Can you hear me Maggie? I love you. I love you…"

Although Sis. Terry was in a coma until the day she died, and could do nothing for herself, he kept her at home. He hired someone full time to watch and care for her. He did not travel much in those years, but he did travel some. He came to Calgary where I started pastoring in 1977. He would call home every day. He used our phone and his conversation was not private. We could not help overhearing what he was saying. He would enquire of the care giver how Sis. Terry was doing. After he had been brought up to date on her condition, he would say, "Now put the phone up to her ear. Hello, Maggie? Maggie? How are you doing? Are they taking good care of you? I miss you. I sure am missing you. I'll be home soon. I'm coming home, Maggie, and I can't wait to see you. Alright, pucker up now, because I'm going to give you a kiss. Are you ready?" And then he would make the sound of a smack into the phone. This was his habit every day when he was not home.

Canada

Bro. Terry was invited to be the day speaker at the Canadian Plains District campmeeting. The District included Alberta and Saskatchewan. One of the things Bro. Terry was appreciated (and unappreciated) for was telling it like it is. He was afraid of nobody but God. His plain-spoken manner of preaching often offended people, and this campmeeting was no exception. In fact, two or three district preachers were so upset that they complained to Bro. Dan Mena, who was the district coordinator. (It was an unorganized district at the time and did not have a Superintendent.) Bro. Mena called a minister's meeting after the evening service and the complainers were allowed to air their grievances. As recording secretary, I was busy taking notes, but I can remember my legs shaking as I had to listen while my pastor was criticized. Bro. Terry was not present in the meeting, he was in his cabin sleeping as sound as a baby. And it was a good thing, too, because this meeting lasted until the sun came up. Nothing came of the complaints, so one of the preachers decided to brace Bro. Terry himself. That was not a good idea, and I think the brother regretted it. Bro. Terry listened to the young man politely. Then, before walking off, he said, "You'd probably make a good trinitarian preacher."

Several Bakersfield boys moved to the Canadian Plains District to start churches. Bro. Ken Bow went to Saskatoon, Saskatchewan (and became my best friend). Bro. Bob Dansby went to Prince Albert, Saskatchewan, Bro. Randy Kendrick went to Regina, Saskatchewan. Bro. Keith McCoy went to Medicine Hat, Alberta, and Melvin Lazenby was in Lethbridge, Alberta. Six Bakersfield boys were too many for one small district. The same men who were upset with Bro. Terry's preaching at campmeeting were furious at Bro. Terry's boys in the district. They could not stand our uncompromising message on doctrine and holiness. We were I.H. Terry's boys, and we had learned our lessons from the master teacher.

Letters began to fly from our little district to St. Louis, the headquarters of the organization. Those who were upset with us sent a steady supply of complaints. A meeting was called. The officials were to come to our campmeeting and this huge problem would be settled once and for all.

Bro. Terry called me and asked what was going on. He said that N.A. Urshan, the General Superintendent, had called him about all the problems 'his boys' were causing. When Bro. Terry found out that the problem was our stand on the absolute essentiality of the New Birth message and standards of holiness, he told me, "There's going to be a meeting. I'll be there, but whatever happens, DON'T BACK DOWN." What I didn't know at the time was that when Bro. Urshan had called him, Bro. Terry had told him, "If they're wrong…get 'em." So, he told Bro. Urshan to get us and told us not to back down.

It was an interesting meeting. Much of the Executive Board was there, including Bro. Urshan, Bro. Becton and Bro. Kilgore. We joked that the district ministers were outnumbered by headquarters officials. When the letter writers were given the chance to speak, they refused to say anything. The delegation from headquarters realized they had been had, and we heard nothing more about these 'problems'.

Bro. Terry and the Organization

Bro. Terry got along well with Bro. Urshan. They were both strong individuals. Both of them commanded attention by their very presence. When they walked into a room, they became the center of attention. Both of them would have preachers standing around just to hear them speak. Bro. Urshan asked Bro. Terry to come to St. Louis and speak to the combined session of the General Board and the Executive Board at the mid-winter meeting of 1987. Bro. Terry's three-hour fifteen-minute message to the leadership of the UPCI has become a matter of record. The recording is widely available and has been listened to countless times. To say Bro. Terry had everyone's attention would be an understatement and might be illustrated by what Sis. Urshan said to Bro. Pugh the next day. Bro. Pugh, an amazing speaker in his own right, taught a message the following morning using an overhead projector. Bro. Pugh (like Nathaniel Wilson) was a visionary who sometimes talked above his audience and left them wondering what he was talking about. This was one of those times. Sis. Urshan said to him, "I don't understand it, Bro. Pugh. Bro. Terry preached over three hours last night and nobody yawned. You only went an hour today and everybody was yawning."

Bro. Terry had a unique relationship with his organization, the United Pentecostal Church International (UPCI). From his conversion, he was part of the Pentecostal Assemblies of Jesus Christ (PAJC). He knew that another organization, the Pentecostal Church Incorporated (PCI) was not strong on the essentiality of the New Birth message. He was strongly against the merger of these two organizations which resulted in 1945 in the creation of the United Pentecostal Church (UPC, and later known as the UPCI). He realized that, even up to the time of his death, the UPCI still had a large contingent of preachers who did not believe that baptism in Jesus' name and the infilling of the Holy Ghost was a heaven or hell issue. In his words, "We're up to our knees with guys who believe that."

In spite of this knowledge, Bro. Terry was loyal to the organization…within limits. For instance, when I was a young man in Bakersfield, he almost never attended a fellowship rally and he didn't advertise them in his church. In fact, the Western District Board gave some of the men from Bakersfield a hard time over that subject when they met the Board to apply for ministerial credentials. He also did not approve of his young men attending bible school. Ray Brown is the only one I can remember who went to bible school, and I don't know if he got the elder's approval for that.

Bro. Terry also had no patience with a UPC preacher who would wear, or let his wife wear a wedding band. He told the UPCI leaders in his headquarters' message, "There will never be unity in the UPC until it is settled whether a woman wearing a ring on her finger is wearing gold." Another "limit" to his loyalty is that Bro. Terry told us, "If the UPC ever accepts television, we are out." Although he was becoming disillusioned with the organization before he died, up until at least 1996 he said, "I have the United Pentecostal Church in high regard and have shown my allegiance...through many difficulties."

I can think of five reasons for his strong feelings of "allegiance." First, his pastor, A.H. Browning, supported the merger and stayed with the UPC. He respected his pastor. Second, Bro. Terry believed in reaching the world with the Gospel. He felt that there was a greater possibility to reach the world with the Acts 2:38 message in a joint effort than as an independent. He believed we could reach further by joining hands, than by standing alone. Third, he had seen many stupidities and abuses practiced in independent churches, at one time known as "Free Pentecost," and it disgusted him. He recognized the potential harm of an "independent" spirit and saw the safety, for himself and his church, in belonging to an organization. Fourth, he genuinely loved many of the men in the UPC who had showed themselves strong on the message. He also was friends of many good men who left the organization to form the Apostolic Ministers Fellowship (AMF), but his friendship with them was not enough to counter his feelings of loyalty to the UPC. Last, and, I think, most importantly, Bro. Terry believed in church government. He believed in accountability and submission. It is what he taught his saints, and he practiced what he preached. He said, "I love the UPC because it gives us structure. If there was a better organization I'd be in it, but the UPC is the best apostolic organization going."

Considering the above, it is my opinion that if Bro. Terry were alive today, and if he were active in the ministry, he would have left the UPCI when that organization reversed its long-held stand against advertising on television and afterward removed the prohibition for ministers to have a television in their homes. I also believe he would have joined another organization as soon as possible. He would not have sought position. He would have sought unity, order, and doctrinal strength and purity. And he would have said, "Let's join together to help missions so we can bring back the King."

I Want Something Nice

In 1996, Steven Carrier published *A Man and a Woman Passed this Way Blessed by God: The Life of Isaac Hilliard Terry.* Carrier had asked me to review the manuscript before it was published. When I told my pastor that Steven Carrier had sent me his manuscript and asked me to read it, he asked, "What'd he write?" I said, "He just wrote the truth." "Truth!" he said, "I don't want truth. I want something nice."

Unique

He was just naturally unique. He didn't try to be someone else and he didn't try to impress others. He was comfortable in his own skin. One pastor I was preaching for said, "Bro. Terry is known far and wide for carrying a pocket knife and wearing brogan shoes. I wish I had something that people would know me by." I told this to Bro. Terry. He thought for a very brief moment and said, "Well, he could let the spit drip from the side of his mouth and run down his face."

From the Trash

Bro. Terry liked to chew on paper. He also liked to doodle. One day, he was looking for a piece of paper to chew or draw on. Not seeing any within reach, he retrieved an envelope from the waste paper basket. He had thrown all his junk mail there. He looked at the envelope he had thrown away. It was something on the business head of an oil well service and supply company. Now, a little more curious than he had been earlier, he wondered what was inside. He opened the envelope and found a check from Stanley Webb. Stanley did not attend church, but his wife and kids did, and Stanley believed in paying tithes. The check from the trash can was written to Bro. Terry for $35,000. I think he went out and bought a new Mercedes Benz, in keeping with his philosophy of having a good car, a good bed and a good pair of shoes.

Sending Laborer's into the Harvest

Bro. Terry did not point men to himself but to Jesus Christ via the apostles. He did not make us disciples of I.H. Terry. He made us disciples of Truth. He sent 40 or more preachers into the harvest by being slow and steady. He didn't get all excited about every new program and method. His method was to preach the Word, teach consistently, (command and teach), and give young men a chance by putting them on the platform and using them periodically to lead a service, lead songs or preach. I've been asked many times to explain how Bro. Terry was able to produce so many preachers. I think the simple answer would be he didn't wait until a man perfected his ministry before using him. He used us when we were green behind the ears. It wasn't the perfect and smooth service he was interested in, it was giving his boys the opportunity to practice and stretch. In addition to an absolutely solid doctrinal foundation, he offered us experience that could only be obtained by on-the-job training.

He believed that if God called you to a place to start or pastor a church, your responsibility was the preach the Word. You were not responsible to build a church. That was God's job. You preach the Word and God will add to the church such as should be saved. He was not saying you don't need to do any outreach. He was constantly in outreach mode. Outreach was a lifestyle with him, and not a program. He simply invited a lot of people to church as he went through life.

We will never forget the simple but beautiful truths he expounded in his doctrinal messages. (They were all doctrinal.) "The 3 Witnesses," "Paul's Gospel," "THE Lord," "Beginning at Jerusalem," "The Man With The Keys." He also preached a lot about the grace of God in messages like "The Judge," "The Author," "The Hounds of Heaven," "God Is Not Ashamed to be Called Their God," and "Will God Abide by His Own Doctrine?"

He was a lover of good men. And good men loved him.

Chapter 6

Kenneth Bow

My introduction to I. H. Terry

I was eighteen years old and had just graduated from High School. I opened the door to First Pentecostal Church of Bakersfield, California not knowing I was also opening the door to my future.

My attention was immediately drawn to the man in the pulpit. As I stepped through the door he threw a song book. I stopped. I had never seen anything like that in church before. Stupidly I just stood there in the aisle captivated by his actions. I. H. Terry was in the pulpit preaching about finances. The stack of song books on the edge of the pulpit represented the bills people owed. As I watched he picked up another book and flung it out into the altar area and said something like "yeah you will pay Sears and Roebuck, but you won't give God a dime."

I was mesmerized. He continued down the list of monthly bills most people had and threw a song book for each of them. Was it impacting? To this day, forty eight years later it is as vivid in my mind as it was in 1970. I had just got a glimpse of the preaching style of I. H. Terry. It grabbed my heart then and there, and I never lost the wonder of his unique style of preaching.

I arrived at First Pentecostal Church as a young married man, eighteen years old. Brother Terry had married us. The next five and a half years were my university in the school of life. Pastor Terry once told me of the Bible school up in Stockton. He said they manufacture them on an assembly line, but I hand finish and polish my preachers. I was hand polished by this incredible man and then sent into the ministry. I would not trade those five and a half years for any formal education in any prestigious university in the world. I am what I am today because of my years of being in I. H. Terry's boot camp.

I feel like my early life was void of strong male leadership. My mother was married several times and none of the men she married ever played any role in my development. When I met Pastor Terry, that role was filled and it was a godsend.

I was only there a short time when Pastor Terry asked me to be youth leader. I was young and barely older than the youth in the youth group. Some of those young men are writing sections in this book. Reverends Dansby and McCoy were both in the youth group at that time and also their future wives. Because we were all so close in age, we kind of grew up together as a youth group.

Adapting to FPC

The adaptation to Pastor Terry's preaching and leadership style was seamless and immediate for me. I loved his ministry and teaching from the first moment. It was truly love at first sight. His preaching was solid and doctrinal without frills or nonsense and yet it was eclectic. That appealed to me.

My adaptation to the First Pentecostal Church was not as quick or easy. I am not, and have never been, an outgoing person so my reticent ways caused me to be slowly integrated. I was asked quickly to teach a Sunday School class and was placed in the classroom with the elder Sister Helen Frost. There were some rowdy teenage boys in that class and I was to provide some "bouncer" like influence. It was a tremendous blessing to be paired with this quiet, soft spoken, godly woman. Her Christianity challenged me to be better. She was one of the finest Christians I have ever known.

The Sunday School Connection

I also was asked to drive a Sunday School bus. I did, and drove a bus until I left to enter full time ministry. This was the most helpful factor in my integrating into the church. The drivers met on Sunday morning for coffee and breakfast and this helped me to get acquainted with several brothers. Brother L. D. Wilson, Brother Gene Powell, Brother Dave Powell, and several others made me feel accepted.

Youth Leader

I was there just a few months and Robert Condren left to go preach. He was the youth leader and when he left Pastor Terry asked me to take the youth over. I was surprised because I had not been there very long, but was happy to help any way I could. I began holding youth services on Tuesday nights and the youth group was a large group. We had a number of events over time and all of this bonded me to the church. We protested the movie "The Exorcist." We went to parks and marched and sang and carried posters. I'm not sure this did any good but it kept us busy. We had some camp outs with some interesting moments. You can get that information from Brother Dansby, but be sure to listen with a grain of salt :))

Young Ministers

Pastor Terry would ask young men to sit on the platform and he would see if they had any "preach" in them. He would walk into the service and point to one young man and say you lead songs and to another, you lead service. If you were asked to lead service you sat next to him in those blue suede chairs. He would dictate to you what to do, who to ask to sing and any other thing he chose. He tolerated no nonsense or false humility. He had this keen sense about shallow stuff. For example if he offered you something and you demurred, or acted humble, he would simply put it back in his pocket. He taught us to be honest and not fake in our humility.

The White Mercedes.

One night when I was sitting next to him in the blue chair leading service he asked me for some paper. He had the habit of eating paper during service. He asked me to get him that envelope he had tossed into the trash can. I got up and got it and handed it to him. He started to take a bite then paused. He looked again at the envelope intrigued. He decided to open it first. He did not recognize the sender. The envelope was from an oil company. We were both shocked when he opened it and there was a check from a sinner man who did not go to our church. The check was for many thousands of dollars. He grinned at me and said I'm glad I didn't eat that I would have gotten indigestion. He told me to read him the letter in the envelope with the check. I read it to him and the man said he was paying tithes so Brother Terry could get a new car. Pastor Terry took that check and bought the white Mercedes car. On a number of occasions when I drove him to preach various places, we would always laugh how he almost ate a Mercedes.

Fellowshipping the saints.

He did not fellowship with the saints that I could see. He came to our house for dinner one time when we invited him. He ate dinner with us and immediately left when the meal was over. He was there if you needed him but he did not intrude or dally to talk of trivial things.

On the other hand he always seemed to enjoy company at his house. When Sister Terry was bed ridden for those many years I visited him often. He always welcomed me. His favorite thing to do in those times was to read poetry. He would read poetry to me by the hour and then he would ask me to read. He corrected me many times on how I was reading it. He would comment it was too fast or to slow or if I stumbled over words. Sometimes he even read it to me and then handed me the book and said now you read it to me.

His genre of poetry was varied. He seemed to like poems that told a story, poems that expressed philosophy of life, humorous poems, and of course he really liked the poems he himself wrote. To me, his love of poetry showed a side of Brother Terry not often talked about by others. I am hard pressed to remember a service that he did not quote some poetry of some kind. Here are a couple examples I remember:

Heights by great men reached and kept
Were not attained by sudden flight
But they while their companions slept
Were toiling upward in the night

Another one:

> He drew a circle that shut me out-
> Heretic , rebel, a thing to flout.
> But love and I had the wit to win:
> We drew a circle and took him In

Public Correction.

Pastor Terry believed in publicly correcting people. Many, many, times he called people's names over the pulpit, mine and my family's included. One time I was working long hours at UPS during the holiday season and I really did need a haircut. In those days the ministry was fighting long hair on men anyway so it did not help that my hair (I actually had hair back then), was over my ears and my collar. I got off work late and got to church in my work clothes. I debated where to sit. I was not really dressed for church but I did not want to register on his radar so I decided to slip in on the platform and sit toward the back row and maybe he would not see me. Well, it did not work. Right in the middle of his sermon, which had nothing to do with hair, he whirled and said Brother Bow come here. I knew I was in the poo-poo. I went up and he turned me around with my back to the audience and grabbed a handful of hair and began jerking my head back and forth. He loudly proclaimed "We will not have this in our church," or something along those lines. I skipped eating lunch the next day and got a haircut on my lunch break.

He would call people down, or tell them to move to another pew, or go get a cup of coffee if they were yawning. He regularly disfellowshipped people. He was just as quick to restore them if they repented. He disfellowshipped a long list of 26 people one Thursday night. They had all gone to a gospel concert. By Saturday night they were all back in fellowship and we rolled on. He was always quick to forgive people.

They tell a story that once , years before I got there, he posted a list of all the people who did not pay tithes on the church bulletin board. He believed in "rebuke before all that others also may fear" 1 Timothy 5.20.

The Rose Moment

Brother Vaughn Morton has made the "Rose Moment" well known and somewhat famous. I also had the introduction to the Rose Moment. It was in the backyard at his house. Without any preamble while just talking pastor Terry pulled out his pocket knife. He leaned over and cut a rose bud and asked me to unfold it. I was unsure if he was serious, but he was. He was quiet while I tried and broke the petals trying to do as I was asked. Finally he used the same knife and cut a beautiful rose. He handed me the rose, recited the poem "Just Let It Unfold," then he turned and walked back into his house and closed the door. He left me standing in the back yard with a rose in my hand, rose petals on the grass, and the words of the poem on the air. I lingered for a while wondering if he would come back out, but he did not. I took the rose and the lesson home with me.

The Office

Brother Brown mentions in his chapter about not always understanding Brother Terry. Shortly after the Rose Moment, Pastor Terry began to ask me to go in the office with him. He would counsel, chastise, or just inquire of things with the saints. This was awkward for both me and the saints. I would sit in the back of the office and mostly listen. There were a few times when he would ask my opinion or what I suggested should be done. I felt inadequate and unqualified in these moments. I deferred to his wisdom and judgment. It was during this time that Pastor Terry began to have people sign the wall of his office if they were called in. One particular man had several signatures on the wall and Pastor suggested the man had his autograph on the wall enough times and he did not want to see the man in the office again. The man never went back in as far as I know. Before I left that day I counted and sure enough, the man's signature was on the wall six times.

Another time I was stunned when Pastor began to accuse a young woman of fornication. She cried and profusely claimed her innocence. Pastor never relented or backed up, he was adamant. He had no inside knowledge, only his wisdom and God speaking to him. I feared there might be backlash if she was not committing fornication, and was being accused. Within the week the news was out that she was several months pregnant. I never saw him miss it in the many times I was in the office.

As suddenly as he started having me in the office, after about six months he stopped. He never mentioned it again. I never understood his rationale.

During this time I observed the parents who stood with Pastor Terry when their kids made mistakes were able to keep their teenagers in church. Every parent that went against Pastor, I watched their kids backslide. This pattern never deviated as far as I know. It taught me that when a parent stands between a Man of God and their child, their child will not respect authority, and will lose out with God. It is a lesson I never want to forget.

Painting His House

One day he asked if I knew how to paint? I said yes I could do that. He took me to his rental house and told me to paint the house and then he would pay me. It took a little over a week to finish. I went to his house and said I was done. He said let's go look. We drove back to the rental. He examined it very carefully. When he was finished looking around he pulled a gun out of his pocket and handed it to me, then got in his little pickup and drove off without a word. I stood there quite a while wondering what I was supposed to do with the gun or if the gun was my payment for painting the house. I assumed the gun was my payment, and nothing else was ever said. These moments were his ways of teaching. He made you make conclusions and think for yourself. It also taught me not to question him. I trusted him fully.

Early Life

Pastor Terry was born on July 19, 1912, so he was 58 years old when I arrived in Bakersfield. He began the church in 1943 so when I arrived he had been there about twenty eight years. He frequently related his testimony during service or during preaching. He came to the Lord under Reverend A. H. Browning in the 1930's. One of the evangelists that preached to Brother Terry was Choice Webb who also came to California and pastored in Porterville. They were long time friends. Many times Bro. Webb would come by our church and sing or preach. It seems to me he always broke a guitar string when he sang. He sang songs like "It's real" and some song about a turkey buzzard sitting on the church steeple or something. The church seemed to always enjoy Bro. Webb stopping by.

Early in his ministry when the church was on 18th street Brother Terry was having trouble with my great uncle and a man named Connie Lynch. As a young pastor Brother Terry would preach and these older more seasoned "ministers" would ask to say something. They would stand and begin to undo what Pastor had just taught. One night when this happened Pastor left the building and started walking down the railroad track. It was there that somehow God told him he was the pastor and to go back and sit those men down and never again relinquish his pulpit.

It was a defining moment in his life. He turned and went back. He entered the building and Jim Barber (my great uncle) was still speaking. Pastor interrupted him and said sit down. Barber protested and Pastor told him if he did not sit down he was going to tell everyone how Barber had lost his finger. Barber sat down and was never an issue again. Barber and Lynch left and sought easier churches to trouble in the Bakersfield area. There seemed to never again be any question who was in charge at First Pentecostal Church. I. H. Terry had learned he was responsible for his flock and to my knowledge, he never again relinquished the final say to another man.

This boldness was a part of his mantra and who he was. I saw it manifested on several occasions when church trouble surfaced. When a powerful young evangelist caused great trouble and a potential church split I saw him rise and take charge. In these moments he was fearless. He never showed a flicker of fear or uncertainty. By the time I arrived those early issues were long settled. He always found great humor that Jim Barber was my great uncle. I made sure he knew you can pick your friends, but your relatives.... well?

Preaching

One of the most under appreciated facets of Pastor Terry was his eclectic style of preaching. Often I have heard of his preaching as doctrinal, and it was much of the time, but make no mistake, he was not one dimensional. He could be straightforward and doctrinal with the reading of many scriptures. He could also preach the intangibles and make you see them in your mind with his ability to paint word pictures.

He would often leave the pulpit and walk the aisles and preach. At times he would use illustrations and include people. He used humor, and wit, and poetry, and history. He would rub his bald head or rub his chin whiskers on the microphone. He had quaint sayings like "eat it saints," or "how readest thou?" He could preach angry or happy or problems. He had this thing he did where he walked down the aisle with his hands forward parallel to the ground and raise and lower them with the palms down. I was never sure what it meant exactly. He was sensitive to the presence of God and always wept easily.

He could make his point in a way that was unforgettable. There was this brother in the church who was maybe not quite up to average. His initials were A. E. One night Brother Terry put A. E. on one side of the platform with a concordance. On the other side of the platform he put all the sharp young ministers with a concordance as well. He preached on wine for communion. He told A. E. every time you find a scripture in the Bible on wine stand and read it. He told the young preachers every time they found a verse on grape juice to stand and read it. It soon was obvious there were many verses on wine and A. E. would proudly stand and read another one. None of the young ministers ever stood to read. Without saying it, what Brother Terry said was in effect, even if you are not up to average, you can see the Bible supports wine for communion. His terminology was "even a dunce" could understand that.

He preached the message on mud slinging (gossip) by slinging mud from a five gallon bucket. He covered walls and people. There was mud in their hair, on their clothes, on the walls. He preached about the heart and brought a stone in the shape of a heart and preached about the word being like a hammer breaking the rock in pieces. He used a hammer and pounded the rock while chips and pieces flew.

If these do not illustrate his being eclectic then what would? He was unique.

The night I got his Bible.

I had left Bakersfield and gone to evangelize and came home for Thanksgiving to be with family. I went to church on Thursday night and Bro. Terry asked me to preach or rather said "you'll be preaching tonight." That was his way with me. After the service I gathered my courage and asked him if I could ask a favor. He seemed surprised and stopped and looked at me with that look that saw more than your countenance. It felt like he was looking inside your thoughts. I popped the question. I told him I would like to have his pulpit Bible that he preached me the gospel from. I was willing to wait if he would promise I could have it. He just looked at me for what seemed a long time then reached over and handed me the Bible. That was all. No speech, no words, nada. He slipped it out of the custom leather cover it was in. The cover was made by a man in Elder C. W. Shew's church. I wanted that too and wondered if I should push my luck knowing his unpredictable ways. I went for broke. I said would you consider giving me the case as well? Same process, long look, reached over and handed the case to me and walked away. He never mentioned it and I sure was not about to.

Years later I was telling Brother Leon Frost about it. I was so thrilled to have it. Brother Frost listened and when I finished he said "He gave me the church." Touché! It is pretty hard to trump that.

After I became pastor in Washington State I learned Sister Myers had Sister Terry's Bible. I started working on Sis. Myers and eventually talked her into that Bible as well. I am blessed to have their two Bibles. In Sis. Terry's Bible are old notes, Sunday school lessons, handwritten notes about some of the revivals, and some photos of her and Sis. Browning.

I consider these two Bibles among my greatest treasures.

The fireworks and the office.

When Pastor Terry on a trip left he usually left a minister in charge. On one trip away he left one of the local men in charge. I arrived at church one Sunday morning and someone told me brother so-and-so wanted to see me in Brother Terry's office. I went and he was sitting behind Brother Terry's desk. He proceeded to work me over pretty good based on something another brother had said about a fireworks stand. The complaining brother had gone to brother so-and-so and told him some bogus information and he was telling me "what for" sitting there behind Brother Terry's desk. I did not mean to be rude but it struck me as funny and I started laughing. This of course made him more angry. It seemed absurd to me him sitting there like he was Brother Terry's envoy or ambassador, so I just walked out. Both of those brothers informed me I was in deep trouble when Brother Terry got home. Well, I happened to be standing in the vestibule when Bro. Terry came home and they were waiting for him. They loudly said "Brother Terry we need to talk to you." He replied "about what"? They said "about Ken Bow." Brother Terry threw back his head and laughed and walked away. That was the last I ever heard about it. He was unpredictable.

Developing preachers

His method of developing preachers was unique to him. He never scheduled me to preach. I would go to church and he would inform me I was preaching that night. There was no notice ahead of time. The first time I preached in the Bakersfield church, the Singing Parkers were singing. They were on their last song and almost finished. Brother Terry turned to me and said "when they finish, you go preach." I had somewhere around 2-3 minutes notice. I did my best. I do not remember many sermons through the years I have preached, but I remember that one. I spoke on "The camel's are coming." It was the story of Isaac waiting for a bride and she rode up on a camel. I was trying to say we are on our way to meet the bridegroom. I was not impressed, but from that moment forward I felt like he was grooming me to go preach.

Then came a night I remember well. He asked me to lead service that night and I reached over and picked up the copy of the Living Bible he kept there for reference. As I randomly opened it, it fell open to a passage in Acts. In that version it said "you are to go everywhere, telling what you have seen and heard." The sensation that overwhelmed me in that moment was powerful and private. I asked Brother Terry if it was time for me to leave and go preach. His answer was, yes it is time. The next day I gave my thirty day notice at United Parcel Service where I worked. I told no one except Brother Terry and my wife I had given my notice. I felt if God was in it, He would open the doors.

I had no place to go, no revivals scheduled and did not know many preachers. I preached that Sunday night and after church Brother Johnny King came to me and said "you need to go preach." I said "I am going." Surprised, Brother King said "when?" I said "in thirty days." He said "where?" And I confessed I had no idea. Brother King had left and was evangelizing and asked if I would like for him to line up some revivals. I said yes and he was able to connect me with one man in Texas for one week.

I pulled out of Bakersfield in July of 1976 and God helped us and we never looked back. We drove over a thousand miles for one week of revival and God opened doors from there. I will always be grateful to Johnny King for helping me get started, because I. H. Terry did not believe in doing that himself. You were literally on your own. To Brother Terry you either sank or swam, and if you had the goods you would make it. He was old school to the core on that point.

The drive.

The year before I left to go preach was a trying year for me. Death has always affected me deeply and through the years it seemed to intensify each time someone died. I went through a season of some type of depression. It was a dark time in my life. It began when an uncle died. Within a short time I had several traumatic events close together.

At work I was involved in an accident. It was not my fault, in fact the California Highway Patrol listed my contributing to the accident at zero percent. The officer assured me it was not my fault in any way. Still, it bothered me. A young man and a passenger were speeding on a motorcycle and hit my delivery truck while I turned left. They were catapulted down the road flipping head over heels and the driver crashed into a parked pickup. His head slammed into the bumper and caved in. They were not wearing helmets as helmets were not required then. Not having a helmet on was a rare exception to the rule, it saved his life. Had he been wearing a helmet it would have broken his neck the medical team said.

Shortly after this my mother was murdered. I was appointed executor of her estate. I was 22 years old. Her current husband had murdered her. He boasted of this on several occasions. My younger sister and brother had to be cared for as they were under age. All of the associated events of her death, her funeral and her estate stretched into months.

These events buried me into an ever growing darker sense of darkness. It reached the place I would just come home and sit in a chair and stare at the walls. I never missed church or work and I kept up the outward appearance of normality. This continued for several months. It was my last and darkest trial before I left for the ministry.

It was a spring day in 1976 before I left to go preach in July. I came home and I knew I needed help. I was sinking deeper and deeper into some kind of darkness. I called Brother Terry. I asked if I could talk to him. He said I could. I asked if I could come right then, and he told me yes.

I drove to the house on 30th street. When I drove up he came out and got into his little red Toyota pickup. I got in. No words were spoken. He started driving. I tried to explain my problem. He listened carefully. I could not make sense. It was jumbled up and disjointed. He remained silent. I remember the moment the darkness left me.

We were going south on Union Avenue. He stopped to turn right on Brundage Ln. I cannot explain this and honestly do not, and have never been able to fully grasp what happened at that moment. I only know the dark cloud and feeling of depression that had settled on me for months instantly lifted. I physically felt it leave me. In that one moment at that corner, all the months of oppression simply disappeared.

It was so powerful I said "Bro. Terry, I'm all right, we can go home." He still never said a word. When we reached his house he got out and went in the house. In all the arrival, the drive, and the return, he never spoke a word to me. Yet the bondage of my mind was gone and has never returned. The spirit that was oppressing me could not stay in the presence of this man of God, my pastor.

I have wondered many times about that drive that day. Somehow I. H. Terry had the wherewithal to gently let me find my way. He stood aside and let me see Jesus, not I. H. Terry. It was truly a defining moment in my life. Neither of us ever spoke of it again.

Could I have climbed out of the morass without him? I don't know, but I did not have to. Brother Terry was there and he knew how to handle the situation. He was a spiritual man and a very wise man. The preacher said in Ecclesiastes 3.7 "a time to keep silence, and a time to speak." I have marveled through the years and many times asked myself how many men would have handled that moment as he did. How many men would have remained silent and let Jesus handle the moment? I am inclined to think not many would have. Brother Terry did, and I have ever been grateful.

Closing thoughts.

Brother Terry had some neighbors that were a little eccentric. I am not sure of all the conversations, but the neighbors poured several colors of paint on a large boulder/rock in his front yard. I think they were being peevish.

Brother Terry left the paint as it was. He did not attempt to clean it off. It stayed like that for a number of years. In these ways he was so unique and unpredictable.

Once years later when I was pastoring I called him. I was teaching on church government and I asked if he had any thoughts I could add to my notes. He listened without interruption and said "you are the church government" and hung up the phone.

Another time I called him and asked if he would come preach for me. He sternly replied "I'll tell you when I need to come preach for you" and hung up the phone. I said to myself ok, wait to hear from him. Several months later I saw him and he asked my why I was not asking him to come preach anymore. I related the conversation and he said "oh don't pay any attention to that." So I didn't and asked him to come several times after that and he willingly came. You just never knew...

I was driving him to Corcoran to preach a fellowship meeting in his white Mercedes. We had stopped at a 7-11 to buy some sen-sen. As we were driving and he was sitting quietly in the passenger seat eating sen-sen I thought it would be a good time to ask what he believed on predestination.

I asked and he just stared straight ahead. After a few miles of further silence I asked again thinking maybe he did not hear me. Well, after another five miles of silence I asked a third time. He turned his head ever so slowly, put a piece of sen-sen in his mouth, and gave me an impish smile. He turned back to staring ahead at the highway and I got the message. What he believed was his business. Either he did not want to speak of it, or for some other reason he did not plan to discuss it. For the record, he never spoke to me of his belief on predestination.

These instances and many other eccentric moments and actions made him different than any person I have ever met. Sometimes there were things not seen by others. For instance, once at a church picnic he was standing with a group of men and Sis. Terry came driving up. Brother Terry informed those men he was going to tell Sis. Terry to go home and not attend the picnic and he let those men know she would not murmur one word of argument.

When she drove up he walked over and she rolled the window down. He leaned into the window and said very loud "Maggie go home, you are not coming to the picnic today." She sweetly said "yes Ike" and drove off. The men were greatly impressed with his ability to have such a submissive wife. It was years later they found out when he leaned into that window he dropped a hundred dollar bill in her lap.

The contrast of the man was colossal. Preach doctrine hard and sure, then turn around preach like the greatest evangelist who ever lived. Be short and curt with the people who were insincere, and then take time with a struggling young man.

He took a stand to stay in the UPCI when his closest friends went AMF. He was fierce and fearless. He was contrite and in total control. He was fair and yet impartial. He would rebuke at the drop of a hat and even drop the hat himself, but he was also quick to tears and forgiveness. He was transparent, yet there were depths in him that seemed without limit. He was provocative yet patient. He was stern yet supportive. He was intelligent yet intuitive. He could be austere, authoritative, and ascetic and yet people came to him and he read sincerity in them, hunger in them for God, and he opened his heart.

Will there ever be another like him?

Would he build a great church in today's world? My vote, my opinion is unequivocally yes. I never saw him out of his element. I never saw him flounder. He drew men to him at conferences. They sought his shadow. They sat at his feet and listened. I believe there were so many dimensions to this incredible giant of Pentecost that no social barrier would have impeded him.

He was called of God.

He was I. H. Terry.

The dream.

I would like to conclude my chapter with a moment that lives in my memory. It was a Thursday night. I think most people are aware of the pastor when he enters the service. They notice if he is smiling or seems burdened. I also noticed Pastor Terry when he came into the church, and I always tried to assess his mood.

This night he was not smiling and walked straight down the aisle to the pulpit. He spoke to no one and did not pause to shake hands with anyone. He did not assign anyone to lead service or songs. He went directly to the pulpit and began to speak without any preliminary.

He told us he had had a dream. He began to describe the dream. It was an audible masterpiece. In his dream he dreamed he went to heaven. He described to us heaven and how it looked. It was an amazing, captivating moment.

He spoke of the mansions, the golden street, the angelic singing, and the euphoric feeling of being with Jesus. In his dream Jesus was showing him around the celestial city. After several minutes of detailed and intriguing dialog, he said in his dream he asked Jesus a question.

In his dream there was everything he had ever hoped there would be in heaven. It was beyond his wildest expectations. But there was one thing lacking. There were no people. The city was empty of any people.

In his dream he turned to the Lord and asked Jesus; "where are the people?"

Jesus turned and looked into Bro Terry's eyes and said "this is when mercy fails."

He preached that night on "when mercy fails."

This too was one of the many colors of the prism that composed the man: I. H. Terry.

He was doctrinal, he was poetic, he was artistic, and he was brilliant.

I agree with Mark Twain that the true biography of a man can never be written.

Like Twain, it can be said of I. H. Terry:

What a wee little part of a person's life are his acts and words. His real life is led in his head and is known to none but himself. All day long and every day the mill of his brain is grinding and his thoughts, not those other things are his history. His acts and his words are merely the visible thin crust of his world, with it's scattered snow summits and its vacant wastes of water. They are so trifling a part of his bulk, a mere skin enveloping it. The mass of him is hidden. His volcanic fires that toss and boil, never rest day or night. These are his life and can never be written. Each day would be a book of 80,000 words, 365 books a year. Biographies are but the clothes and buttons of the man. The biography of the man himself can never truly be written.

Chapter 7

Robert Dansby

Sometime ago I was out of state visiting with a group of pastors, while talking about the work of God, the topic of building a church came up. As usual, in a setting such as this, the topic of Bro. I.H. Terry came up. The questions were asked, how did he do it, what did he do. For the next hour or so we talked about the **Man**, the **Preacher**, my **Pastor**, I.H. Terry. As we did past memories of my pastor flooded my thoughts.

The problem of writing about Bro. Terry has nothing to do with lack of content, it's what do we put in and what do we leave out, (**For those who were close to, and loved Bro. Terry there should be a few hidden chapters**), also where does one start? Each one of Bro. Terry's men has a personal story to tell about this Icon within the Apostolic Pentecostal movement.

As I reflect back on the past years, I want to state that it was a privilege and honor to be raised in the Bakersfield Church under the leadership of this GREAT, ONE OF A KIND MAN OF GOD.

I was born and raised in the Bakersfield Church. For a few years we went to Bro. Lee Davis' Church in Riverside, where I was baptized and received the Holy Ghost. Moving back to Bakersfield was the best move that could have happened for me. Bro. Terry was a figure that was always larger than life, he was at times very intimidating, yet at the same time he was very kind and compassionate to children. As kids growing up in the Bakersfield

Church, we thought First Pentecostal Church at 36 & 0 was the center of the universe. We felt sorry for all the others who had to attend church elsewhere, such as Fresno, Modesto, Stockton, San Diego and San Jose. I guess this is why people such as Sis. Debbie White gives us a hard time about Bakersfield, calling it Mecca.

My early memories of Bro. Terry were of a man of God like stature, who was all knowing and all powerful. As I grew older I began to understand who he was and what he was. He was the **man** God called and sent to Bakersfield, California for such a time as this. After he retired and was in his mid-80s, he told me he could never build a church in today's world with his personality. I want to say again; thank God for Bro. Terry's influence and handprint on my life.

Bro. Terry was known as a man who produced preachers. What many do not know, was that Bro. Terry was a very dynamic preacher himself. He could keep one on the edge of their pew and we could list messages that will never be forgotten, such as, You Paid Too Much For Your Whistle, Hounds Of Heaven, I'm Not Ashamed To Be Called Your God, Sign Your Note and many others. While he was a dynamic preacher, he was better known as a doctrinal Bible teacher.

Bro. Terry was a lover and student of the Word of God. He had a simple confidence in the scripture and what it said. He would often say, "how readest thou?" I remember sitting on Thursday and Saturday nights while he would get out the old fashion pull down white window shade. He had all his scripture written on them. It was from these he would teach the basic doctrines of the Godhead, New Birth, Holiness and many other subjects. Bro. Terry put this into the young men he was preparing for the ministry.

Bro. Terry never doubted his calling as a preacher. He **strongly** believed that God ordained his life and destiny. Not long after we came to Grants Pass, Bro. Terry came to see us. I woke **early** one morning to the sound of Bro. Terry stirring around, so up I got and went into the living room. It was one of the best things I have ever done. I fixed Bro. Terry his tea and we set there visiting. It was not long into our visit that Bro. Terry began to tell his personal testimony of how he came to God and about starting the church in Bakersfield. For the next 3 hours I sat spellbound as he wove the details of this incredible journey. It was one of those times when you would have given any amount of money to capture it on a recorder, but to do so would of broke the spell, so I listened mesmerized. On another occasion, after we had built our first building, he came back to preach for us. I'll never forget what he preached, (I Had To Go There To Get Here). Our church set spellbound as we listened to the Elder talk about the path God took him on to bring him to where he was.

It was after he went back home that I received a call from him. He said "Bob I have something for you, but you have to come to Bakersfield to get it." Needless to say, I went. What he gave me was a creation of his about fishers of men (priceless). A large drawing he drew of faces inter-locked and overlaid with a large fish hooks. It was hand written, signed and dated by my pastor with the words, "TO BOB DANSBY A FISHER OF MEN." I brought it home and had it professionally framed. Today it hangs in my office. There has been many a tear shed as I reflect on what it meant, also what it means to me. I felt for the first time I'd finally received the approval and blessing of my pastor.

Bro. Terry was a man many did not understand. Even those of us who were under his leadership did not always understand him, but we loved him. For example, I was the assistant youth leader, I was faithful, I was there for every youth function, I was involved. I was excited and expecting to be promoted to youth director when the time came. The current youth director was leaving, I was excited, thinking I'd step in and take over, but that didn't happen. Bro. Terry never talked to me about it, I learned through my best Friend Bro. Keith McCoy that Bro. Terry had picked him to fill the position. The problem was, Bro. McCoy didn't even come to youth functions. Bro. McCoy remains my closest friend to this day. No I did not understand Bro. Terry's decision, but I continued to love him, he died before I could muster the courage to ask him why he did it.

Bro. Terry was unique, he did things different yet built a powerful church. The first time I went to a AMF meeting I was prepared to be slammed for being in the UPC. I had heard horror stories about their meeting. Nothing unusual happened, and the worship and preaching was excellent. After service I mentioned to one of the officials of the AMF that I was surprised, saying, if this is as bad as it gets, this is nothing, we set through tougher than this on a regular basis in Bakersfield, the officials response was, it is not over.

For years the Bakersfield church was used for pre-conference service when a youth convention was held in town. On one such occasion, my brother Harold and I had a friend with us from Riverside. This teenager was always heavy, at the time he weighed somewhere between 350 and 400 pounds. Before service started we were in the foyer of the church talking when Bro. Terry came up. He stopped and looked Ken up and down, reached down and gripped one of his legs and said, "if I was raising Steers you'd be just the size I'd want." He turned and walked off. Harold and I stood there shocked, while Ken busted out laughing.

After Bro. Terry married my aunt Nita, my mother went to live with Bro. and Sis Nita Terry. Bro. Terry would have my mother put out the Do Not Disturb Sign on the front door so he could take a nap without being disturbed. It was on one of these occasions that the doorbell rang, mother went to the door and standing there was Bro. Murrell Ewing. He asked if Bro. Terry was there? Mother responded yes, he just laid down but he's not asleep, I'll get him up. She knocked on Bro. Terry's door and said, Bro. Murrell Ewing is here to see you. The voice on the other side of the door replied, "can't he read the do not disturb sign?" Bro. Terry and Bro. Ewing did not visit on that occasion, yet Bro. Ewing continued to love Bro Terry. Bro. Terry went through a season when he would stop the visiting preacher and question them as they were preaching, I remember him doing this many times. On one occasion Bro. Phil White was holding a revival, He had heard horror stories from his brother-in-law about Bro. Terry doing this.

Bro White determined he will not do this to me. I'll never forget as Bro. White was preaching, with Bro. Terry setting on the front pew, after a while his hand shot up, he kept it up. Bro. White saw him out of the corner of his eye and turned the other way, determined Bro. Terry would not do this to him. Bro. Terry just kept his hand up. After a time Bro. White began to feel bad, thinking I'm just a young man, that's the Elder, so who am I to refuse him. So Bro. White finally stopped preaching and turned to Bro. Terry and said, "yes Bro. Terry, what do you want?" Bro. Terry acted like he was shocked, and responded and said, "can't an old man just worship God?" A stunned, yet relived Bro. White later said Bro. Terry knew what he was doing.

The Bakersfield Church had powerful, deep moves of God, yet few were the services where there was not preaching, Bro. Terry believed that the most important part of any service was the preaching or teaching. One time a family group came by for a Thursday - Sunday meeting. The first three services the group just sang, no preaching. Bro. Terry knew the father was an outstanding preacher, so on Saturday night at the conclusion of service, remember this was the third night without preaching, Bro. Terry as he was dismissing the service looked back at the preacher and said, "Bro. _____, tomorrow morning you will be preaching," to which the preacher replied, "Bro. Terry I have to obey the Holy Ghost." Bro. Terry shot back, "you'll obey me, I pastor this church." The next morning, the visiting preacher ever more preached. That was over 40 years ago and I still remember the message. (Sissies and Softies Can't inherit the Kingdom of God -1 Cor. 6:9)

Bro. Terry would use his young men to read scripture during his preaching and teaching. One night as he was preaching he told each of us to get a certain verse and be ready to read it when he called for it. One young man, who had a high tenor voice was given a verse, when his time came to read, his high tenor voice shocked Bro. Terry. Bro. Terry stopped, turned to the young man and said, "if I was you I'd catch a cold and keep it" and kept on preaching. The young man is still living and working for God today. Once during preaching Bro. Terry happened to look back and saw a man behind him yawning. Bro. Terry stopped his preaching and said, "Bro. _____, get up and go get a drink," which he did. Bro. Terry did not resume preaching until the man was back on the platform, then he resumed as if nothing out of the ordinary had happened.

In the 70s Bro. Terry was having a problem with some of the younger ladies and teenage girls wearing skirts too short. One service night Bro. Terry was sitting on the steps of the church. If the ladies or girls who walk past him had a hemline that was to short, he would reach out with a black magic marker and put a mark on their leg and say, "next time it's to be down to the mark." My wife to be (Kathy Wilson) was one who received the mark, we have had many laughs about that over the years.

Bro. Terry was a home body, he did not travel much, nor did he preach out much. However, his ministry was far reaching and it had an impact worldwide. After Bro. Terry passed to his eternal reward, Bro. Morton came by to preach for us. I will never forget the message he preached to our local church (THE LESSONS OF LIFE I LEARNED FROM I.H. TERRY). We sat spellbound as the Elder related one story of life after another.

I'll never forget the year 1982, while in Canada involved in home missions. My youth and ignorance got me into trouble, not only did it get me in trouble, it involved Bros. Johnny King, Ken Bow and Dan Mena. As a result of this incident, the Executive Board of The UPCI came to our Camp Meeting to have a meeting, I was the target. One official stood and for a good while ripped me apart without using my name. After he was done I raised my hand and ask Bro. N. A. Urshan if I could speak. He gave permission and it was a wrong move on my part. I stood and said, I'm the one he's talking about, and began to relate my side of the story. I had not said much before Bro. Terry said, "BOB WE DO NOT RECEIVE AN ACCUSATION AGAINST AN ELDER WITHOUT TWO OR THREE WITNESSES." I said Bro. Urshan I withdraw everything I just said and sat down. It was at this point I saw my pastor Bro. Terry go to work, in his own intimidating way he began to question the official, it wasn't long before he had the official very nervous. Bro Terry did not have a fear of men. It was in this same meeting a local pastor accused Bro. Terry of saying something while preaching that Bro. Terry said he didn't say. The local pastor said I have it on tape. Bro. Terry said produce the tape, if you can I'll give you five hundred dollars. The pastor could not produce it. I'll never forget my pastor's remarks. He said "Bro. Urshan this man is trying to make me out to be a_____ a_____ a_____ a_____ a BURRO."
I'll use one of Bro. Terry's saying, go learn what that means.

I want to say again how indebted I am to this MAN, PREACHER, my PASTOR, Bro. I.H. Terry. There will never be another like him, nor would we want there to be. I'm forever thankful and grateful that God allowed me to become one of his sons in the gospel. Twenty-two years ago I was on the phone with a man whom I love deeply, this man does not live for God. As we talked he began reflect on the problems he had in life, and blamed three men, two of which I will not name. He told me, all the issues and problems I have in life, I blame on these three men, one was Brother Terry. After listening to the hate for a while, I'd had enough. I responded saying, I blame them for the way I turned out also. (Those same three men were the three who had the most influence in my life). I said concerning the two unnamed, they are responsible for helping me live for God, and I also blame Bro. Terry for the way I turned out. He put the gospel and the love for it into me.

Did Bro. Terry ever bust my hide spiritually? I still bear in my spiritual body the marks. Thank you Pastor Terry, you never gave up on me even when others did. You were always there with exactly what I needed, rebuke, correction, chastisement or encouragement. Without you I would not be where I'm at today.

Chapter 8

Keith McCoy

As I set at my desk preparing my message for the evening service, I looked up and the picture of Bro. Terry that sits on my desk caught my attention, and I began to think about how he had taught me the word of God, "Take heed unto thyself, and unto the doctrine; continue in them: for in doing this thou shalt both save thyself, and them that hear thee." I said to the picture as if I was talking to Bro. Terry, "Elder I'm still preaching the word of God that you taught me." I've thought back on the experience of that day and realized just as the writer of Hebrews said of Able "he being dead yet speaketh." Bro. Terry is no longer with us, yet his life, walk with God and messages still speak to me.

Sometime after this experience I called my Sister Phyllis that attends the Bakersfield church to get me some of Bro Terry's messages. The first one I listened to was, The Three P's (Peter Paul and Philip) it just so happened that the readers he used for this message from 1980 was Bro Dansby (Paul), Bro. David Lazenby (Philip) and I was (Peter), Bro. Rustin was the 1980 Trinitarian preacher, it brought back a lot of memories of sitting under Bro. Terry's ministry.

In the late 1950's and early 1960's my four uncles and two sisters and their families were attending Bro Terry's church. At about the age of eight, I either rode a bus or was picked up by one of my relatives to attend services from time to time. It was during one of these times I received the Holy Ghost and Bro. Terry baptized me. When I was 12 my mom and dad came to church, mom prayed thru, dad received the Holy Ghost and I prayed through. Within a year or so our family backslid.

In 1970 my future wife Becky and I decided to go to church. I prayed thru the first night and Becky received the Holy Ghost one month later. It was the experiences of my younger years that kept drawing me back. Even though I lived in a backslider's home, I feel so blessed that God allowed me at a young age to experience his love and the ministry of Bro. Terry. I did not realize then the major role that Bro. Terry would play in my life.

Bro. Terry was a firm believer in the scripture that says "try the spirits whether they are of God." He often told the story of when he was over a fellowship meeting how that just after a preacher began to preach, Bro. Terry told him to sit down. After service the preacher came to Bro. Terry and asked him why he sat him down. Bro. Terry said the Bible says," try the spirits whether they are of God." One night Bro. Terry was getting ready to dismiss service he said "if I have not given you a knife see me after church," so after service I went to him and said Bro. Terry, you've never given me a knife. He looked at me and said "I've given you a knife" and turned and walked away. I only received one knife from Bro. Terry and that was when I was leaving to start my first church in Canada.

Around 1978 when I was 24 I began to feel the call to preach. After a few months of praying and seeking God I told God, if this is really what you want me to do then have Bro. Terry call me out in church to sit on the platform. Within a week or two on a Sunday night as he was dismissing service he said "Bro. McCoy, Thursday night I want you in a suit and on the platform." I did not own a suit so I went to Montgomery Ward and bought two suits.

The next Thursday night I walked in the door on the right side of the church, the lights were dim for prayer and right in front of me stood Bro. Terry. We began walking down the aisle toward the platform as he began to inform me I was to lead service that night. I was very shy and had never been on the platform for anything other than dedicating my two boys. As we continued down the aisle I began to beg, please Bro. Terry, let me wait a few nights. As we reached the platform stairs he said you are leading service tonight and walked away. Bro. Bob Dansby led songs that night and after service Bro. Dansby told me, (and I must say he enjoyed telling me), that before service Bro. Terry told him to be ready in case I dropped the ball.

After I had been sitting on the platform for a year or so I felt a burden to get some organized outreach going. At the time we had no outreach director so I went to Bro. Terry and asked if I could start some outreach. He said yes, so I had some meetings with those interested and made plans to go out on outreach. After a few weeks during service one night Bro. Terry asked Bro. Jess Parker to come up to the pulpit and said, "Bro. Parker is our outreach director." He never informed me that he was replacing me before or after that service. I didn't ask and he didn't tell.

It was these kind of experiences that come to mind when he would say " I tried to run you off but you wouldn't leave." He tried our spirits, he tested us to see what we were made of. If we could not handle Bro. I. H. Terry's boot camp then we could not handle what we were going to face in the ministry. I survived.

In 1981 after a family vacation to Canada I asked Bro. Terry if I could leave and start a church in Medicine Hat, Alberta, Canada. At that time four other men were in Canada from the Bakersfield church. Bro. Terry said I had to wait another year and that some of us were going to fail. This was not encouraging news to hear for a 28 year old young man that thought he was going to have nothing but revival in Medicine Hat. About a year later I again decided to ask Bro.Terry if I could leave. So one evening while picking my wife up at his house from taking care of Sis. Terry I thought I would ask. But between phone calls, and people stopping by, disappointed I gave up and decided to go home. When we got home the phone rang. It was Bro. Terry. He wanted to let me know it was time I could leave.

Before we were to leave Bro. Terry called and asked us to come by his house. While we were there he said "I want to give you something." He gave my boys Brian (9 years old), and Brent (7 years old), some marbles that he had when he was a boy, and gave each one a knife. He then again went to the locked room that was by the kitchen and came out with Remington 1100 shotgun and a knife for me. Then he told my wife that he had something for her and that she could never sell it and that she could let me use it but could not give it to me. He walked back to the locked room. We were trying to figure out what could he give my wife that I would want to use. He came out carrying a 30/30 rifle and gave it to her.

It was in October of 1982 we left for Medicine Hat. While in Medicine

Hat Bro. Terry visited us. One night we had a special service and invited the Lethbridge church to join us. I was excited to have him preaching for us and was looking forward to the message until I realized I was the text for the night. He preached "get off the toilet" because he wanted me to find a building to buy even though I only had one family in the church. He repeated that statement several times in the message. For the remainder of his visit we looked for a building to buy. During the same visit Bro. Terry was playing checkers with Brian and said to him "you know what to do if your losing?" Brian said "no." Bro. Terry flipped the board and all the pieces went flying. The boys looked shocked, followed by laughter.

In 1985 we began pastoring in Lancaster, Ca. Because we were only 85 miles from Bakersfield, Bro. Terry would preach for us several times a year. He would call me early on a Sunday morning and say "do you have a preacher this morning?" I would respond "yes Bro. Terry it is you." Our church was blessed to hear some of his classics.

Once when he came he walked out into our vestibule, and when he came back in he was wearing a judges wig. We all had a good laugh then he preached about God standing up to judge. Another time after preaching for us I handed him his check. The same amount as usual and the normal amount that most churches were paying. He said this is not even enough money to pay my gas to get here. The next time he came I paid him twice as much.

One Sunday morning after service he asked me to take him by a church of an elder that he had known which had passed away several years before and the elder's son that was not a preacher was trying to keep it going. Bro. Terry followed me in his car. I thought he just wanted to drive by and see the building but as we were driving by he turned into the parking lot and went inside the building. By the time I caught up with him he was talking to two ladies, one of which was the wife of the son trying to keep the church going. I heard him say, Bro. McCoy here is a pastor and has a group of people but no building and you folks don't have a pastor but you have a building, why not combine the two? Both of the sisters let him have it and told him they did not appreciate him and his idea and told him to leave, so he walked out and I followed.

One of the last times Bro. Terry came to preach for us he brought his future wife with him. They walked in late to service. I motioned for him to come to the platform. I had never met her before so I said "Bro. Terry, I would like to welcome her to our church, what is her name?" He looked at me, then began to laugh and reached in his pocket pulled out a piece of paper with her name Barbara written on it and handed it to me, then we both laughed. They say the memory is one of the first things to go.

He never took me to the dump, but I remember one day he pulled into Bethel in his truck and started passing out never been opened packages of Wrigley's gum that covered the bottom of his truck bed that he found at the dump.

One night while he was preaching he had all the young men come down to the second row of pews and stand facing the congregation while he checked to see if we needed a haircut. When he got to me he said "Bro. McCoy you need a haircut."

Bro David Webb told me that he asked Bro. Terry why he no longer pulled young couples aside that were dating and ask them if they had been kissing or holding hands. He said "I made liars out of the previous generation, no reason to make liars out of this one."

I can still see him walking the aisle with tears running down his face trying to reach another soul preaching "I go a fishing." Yes, he could be hard and untactful, but if you could look past his personality weaknesses you would find a man that loved people. No matter where he was or who he was with, he was always teaching, always reaching, trying to help someone be saved. I heard him as he was walking down the aisle with a visiting preacher say "if you continue going like you are you will be charismatic." The preacher didn't listen.

Bro. Terry was a father to us. He was a master at teaching the word of God in a way that you would love it and we were begotten by the gospel he preached. The older I get the more thankful I feel to have had Bro. Terry as my pastor and spiritual father.
Thank you Bro. Terry for trying my spirit and pushing a shy young man to do what he never thought was possible, for loving me enough to preach to me the truth. By God's grace, I'm going to continue preaching the word of God that you taught me.

Brother Terry you are a legend — and I am a part of your legacy.

Chapter 9

Henry Buczynski

Coming to know and being influenced by Bro. Terry has greatly impacted my life. After I graduated from high school in Erie, Pa. in 1972, I enlisted in the United States Air Force. I was stationed at Vandenberg near Lompoc, Ca. I was witnessed to by Bill Leonard, who went to church in Lompoc, pastored by Bro. Nolan Brooks. I fell in love with this truth.

After I had been in church for about a year and a half, I married Debbie Weese in 1974 at Bakersfield, Ca. This was my first time to meet Bro. Terry. I had met Debbie at a fellowship meeting in our section. She and others from Lancaster were there. At the time she was attending church in Lancaster, pastored by Bro. Eckels. Sis. Eckels is my wife's aunt.

When we got married, Bro. Terry took me into his office to show me his bowling ball with a chain attached. Our photographer said he got a lot of ideas from Bro. Terry. Some of these pictures are in the book Bro. Carrier wrote about Bro. Terry. After we married, I was still in the Air Force and we lived in Lompoc. When I got out of the Air Force, I told my wife I wanted to go to bible college. Debbie told me there was one in Bakersfield. What? I had never heard of one there. She said Bro. Terry's "school" was better than any bible college.

We moved to Bakersfield in August 1974 and my studies began; in rides to the dump, to learn about life, battles we face and what to do in certain situations. For awhile I didn't have a job and Bro. Terry hired me. One day he asked me, "Bro. Buczynski, have you ever been fired?" I said, "No, Sir. I haven't." He said, "You are now." I went home thinking what am I going to tell my wife. The next morning Bro. Terry called and said, "Where are you?" I said, "Bro. Terry, you fired me." He replied, "I just wanted you to know how it felt. I was just testing you and letting you experience what it is like to be fired."

"Give me your minds" was said often as he preached. My children still remember certain messages there. They were dedicated to the Lord by Bro. Terry, as well as my wife when she was a baby. One particular message was about Noah and the ark. Bro. Terry had three couples come up to be Noah's sons and wives. We were one of those couples. He portrayed himself as Noah and would have us work on the ark and then we would sing a song he made up. "We shall ride the waves, we shall ride the waves, when the rain is falling, we shall ride the waves." Then back to working on the ark and then the song again. Our girls still talk about that.

Sometimes, he would call a fellowship meeting on a Saturday night. We had Saturday night services back then. After song service, he would "You, you and you," pointing out three young men to preach. He believed in "Instant in season and out of season." Sometimes he would say "One, two, three" pointing out three to be preaching that night. And you went in the order he said. There was no time to fret…. Preach the word.

Bro. Terry could not sing and said so himself but he used to sing a chorus he made up. It went like this….. "There was joy in the house the night I was born and the joy in the house was for me. O, there was joy in the house the night I was born and the joy in the house was for me."

When we moved to Kansas, we put three verses to it.

Verse 1. In Psalms 87 and verse 5 of Zion it shall be said, that this man and that man was born in her and the highest shall establish her.

Verse 2. I was bought by the blood, sanctified by the word, I was baptized in Jesus Name. I am free my sins, so happy within, for I have found great peace.

Verse 3. The angels danced all over heaven, the night that Zion travailed, repentance brought forth fruit and joy filled my heart for I'd sold all and bought the truth.

Buy the truth and sell it not. Bro. Terry was a word preacher. No flowery sermons, no sad story to move you. You just fall in love with the truth. He said it often, "You need to fall in love with the word."

He would tell the young men, aspiring to be preachers, to go downtown to preach on a corner. Chester Avenue was main street, so off we would go. He said take your wife with you to sing or play.

We helped Bro. Eckels in Shafter 1986 - 1988 and Bro. Terry came to a service and said, "Bro. Buczynski, I heard you are moving to Kansas to start a church. Do you have a job? Your wife and babies are going to starve." He had been after us to do something for awhile so we were ready to go and he was concerned. He really cared about his people. I had a job in exactly two months and will retire from this same job in December of this year (2018). God has been good.

After we had been in Kansas a couple of months, Bro. Terry called. We were so excited to hear from him. I said, "Bro. Terry, I tell everyone I meet about you." It got real quiet on the phone for a few seconds and then Bro. Terry said, "Bro. Buczynski, are you preaching I. H. Terry or Jesus Christ and Him crucified?" I answered, "Bro. Terry, I am preaching Jesus Christ and Him crucified."

I wouldn't trade anything for the wonderful teaching I have been given by this great man of God. The trips to the dump, or the spur of the moment talks that would come up, are priceless.

Bro. Ken Bow has got his arrow and has hit the target in his title for the book; Legend and Legacy. I want to thank all the other ministers and may God bless their endeavors.

.

Envoi

by Vaughn Morton

First, I want to say that I count it an honor to be asked to contribute to this book concerning Elder I. H. Terry. Bro. Booker and myself were not one of "his boys" or should I say one of the preachers from his ministry. So, thank you for asking me.

My story with Bro. Terry starts back in the late 1950's. The first time I ever saw him was at the old Frazier Park Camp Meeting. I never really got acquainted with him until the late 1960's. I was a young man in my late 20's. I had evangelized for seven years and had pastored for three years. Circumstances of life had caved in on me…and that was where I was at. Some brethren told me that Bro. Terry said, "That young man, Vaughn Morton, is really going through it. If he's a good man, let's help him. If he's not, this a good time to get rid of him." I am so glad that he decided to take me in. He treated me as Leviticus 19:34 states, "But the stranger that dwelleth with you shall be unto you as one born among you, and thou shalt love him as thyself." Remember, I was not one of his men, but he took me in.

The three greatest men in my life are my pastor Bro. J.E. Rode, Elder Paul Price and Elder I. H. Terry. They each played a different role. These men helped me along during the trial of my life.

How do you explain someone like Bro. Terry? He is the most unique man I have ever met. He was a character. He was fearless and bold. He was so interesting to me that I listened to over 100 of his tapes. He started the church in Bakersfield from scratch. He built a strong one God, Jesus Name, Apostolic Church. How had he become so successful? Surely, it wasn't his personality. I concluded that he had faith if he preached the Word of God, then God would honor His Word. Bro. Terry was a great Bible teacher. God honored him for loving His Word.

Bro. Terry was very, very strong on the Acts 2:38, One God, holiness within, holiness without and separation from the world message. I think that California was strong in the new birth message because of men like Bro. I. H. Terry and Bro. Jimmy Davis. There is one thing that they really agreed on and that was the Apostolic message. California is a better place concerning the new birth because of them. When a man like Bro. Terry dies, it is like the city library burning down. All that wisdom, knowledge, experience, and history goes with them.
Job 12:2 says, "Wisdom shall die with you."

Some think Bro. Terry to be ruff and tuff, and he could be, but he was also loving and compassionate. He proved that to me by taking me in. As I have already said, he came into my life in my late 20's and for the next 30 something years he worked on me. I made up my mind that I was going to submit to this good elder. It was not always easy because he could be as ruff as cobb.

As most of you already know, he is the one that taught me the lesson that I have been teaching for years, "Just Let It Unfold." If you remember the story, he took me in his backyard, cut a rose bud off, placed it in my hands and said, "Bro. Morton, unfold that rose bud." I tried but I couldn't. When I got through, he said, "That is the way your life is going to be in the end. Nothing but broken pieces because you are trying to force life to unfold it like you want it, instead of yielding to God and letting Him unfold your life." Then he placed in my hands a beautiful rose and said, "God unfolded this rose. It is beautiful, and it has a fragrance. That is the way your life can turn out if you will just relax and let God unfold it."

Just Let It Unfold

It is only a tiny rosebud,
A flower of God's design:
But I cannot unfold the petals
With these clumsy hands of mine.

The secret of unfolding flowers,
Is not known to such as I;
The flower God opens so sweetly
Would in my hands fade and die.

If I cannot unfold the rosebud,
This flower of God's design
Then how can I think I have wisdom
To unfold this life of mine.

So I'll trust in Him for His leading,
Each moment of everyday;
And I'll look to Him for His guidance
Each step of the Pilgrim Way.

For the pathway that lies before me,
My heavenly Father knows;
I'll trust Him to unfold the moments
Just as He unfold the rose.

Here are some lessons he taught me:

- He called me one day and said, "Bro. Morton don't get bitter. I heard some men talking, and they are going to cut you out." Then he read me this poem:
  He drew a circle that shut me out –
  Heretic, a rebel, a thing to flout.
  But Love and I had the wit to win:
  We drew a circle that took him in!
  　　　　　　　　-Edwin Markham

Bro Terry said, "When they cut you out, love them. Draw a big circle and take them in.

- One time I asked Bro. Terry, "What have you done to live as long as you have?" At that time, he was 85 and all he said was, "Be Happy."
- He said, "If you get mad at everything you feel like getting mad at, you will stay mad all the time."
- Concerning money, he said, "When you get your check, give God his tithe. Save some. Eat some-buy groceries. Give some away. If you eat it all, you are a glutton. If you give it all away, you are a fool. If you keep it all, you're an old miser." He also said, "If you want to save money, stay away from fast women and slow race horses."
- One day he told me, "You got a young mind. It is sharp. You can remember. To balance that, he said, "You haven't got much wisdom, but you will get more as you get older."
- Oh yes, any of you that have been around him know that he taught us that every man ought to have a pocket knife. If you don't know what that means, Bro. Terry would say, "Go learn what that means."
- He also said, "Don't judge a man or a woman before their time. Give them time to prove themselves because somewhere, somehow, someway, sometime a man or a woman comes to what they really are. As you see them today they may be what they really are, but in time they may come to what they really are.
- I was standing with him one day, when he said to the president of the Bible College, "You put them out like Ford's and Chevrolets. There's a lot of Ford's and Chevrolets, but the ones I put out are like Rolls Royce…carefully put together."
- Remember he's the one that taught us – "Don't get upset over things that don't really count. It's just water on the ground."
- Oh Yes, he told us to get a good pair of shoes, a good bed, and a good car because if you are not in one, you are in the other.
- And he taught us, it takes a long time to get a gate. Meaning, be patient. It takes a long time to get carpet on the floor, to get a fence, a cement driveway. Don't lose your soul and lay out of church working trying to get your gate. Etc. … you get the idea.
- He also taught us preachers I Tim 4:11, "These things command and teach. Meaning don't just teach them, (to urge, to enjoin, to give charge, to declare) command them. Some men teach, but they do not command.

There are many other things that Bro. Terry taught us, but time and space will not allow us to talk about it. I had the privilege of being of being with Bro. Terry three days before he passed away. His mind was very sharp I had no idea that in three days he would be gone. He said (It was very touching.), "Just think that a little old man like me, in a little old house, in a big old city, and God revealed the truth to me."

We have all been blessed because a man and a woman by the name of Bro. I.H. & Sis. Maggie Terry passed our way.

I want to say in closing, thank you, Bro. Terry, for the memories.

You will forever be in our hearts.

www.ingramcontent.com/pod-product-compliance
Lightning Source LLC
Chambersburg PA
CBHW020128130526
44591CB00032B/576